my daughter, *myself*

'Every now and again a book comes along that leaves me breathless. Connie Easterbrook's book on motherhood, love, loss and life is one such book. At times it literally, not just metaphorically, took my very breath away. With brutal honesty and raw emotion, Connie covers unanswerable questions, such as "How can you be the mother you want to be when you didn't get the mothering you needed?", "How can you unconditionally love a child who frustrates the living daylights out of you?", "How do you come to terms with the reality of the death of a child?" and "How do you ever forgive yourself for arguing with your child on the day before they died?"

'Connie guides her grateful readers forward, by sharing the way she navigated through the quagmire herself. But the story doesn't stay or end here. Connie also shows that it is still possible to lead a meaningful life filled with joy and contentment alongside the companion of crushing and debilitating grief. Not easy, but possible. If you have your own unanswerable questions, you may well find your answers here. Be ready to be left breathless.'

Gay McKinley, *author, counsellor, psychotherapist, facilitator*

'Connie's book will inspire and encourage all her readers. In her real, raw and passionate way, she shows that despite the most difficult losses in life, you can grow and heal. After very hard work, Connie has transformed her suffering into meaningful growth. She has become my teacher in grief and trauma as a friend and as a professional. She is my role model for resilience and hope. May she inspire you, too.'

Beaté Steller, *Accredited Mental Health Social Worker*
M.A.P.S. M.A.Ed B.S.W. (Hon) R.N.

'With the insight of a therapist attuned to her own acute struggle with her daughter's death, Connie explores how the ways that we respond to grief are guided by our lived experience and prior losses – weaving a thread through the lives that touch and encompass our hearts. A meditative, raw and much-needed book.'

Samantha Forbes, *therapist, BA Psychology,*
Master of Counselling Social Work

'Connie has bravely written with sensitivity, honesty and great personal insight about her journey of healing from traumatic grief. Through her parenting challenges, we … discover how parents can find ways to embrace the creative and loving qualities of their own children. She brings together current research into mental health and neurodiversity, whilst reminding us all to truly value the time we have with our loved ones. Her healing journey has produced one of the most powerful pieces of writing I have read on these topics.'

Sonya Bradford, *psychologist and mother of two children with learning difficulties and anxiety*

'It fills me with great pride to be part of a movement where addressing our experiences of grief and loss is accepted as the new normal. Connie and her heartwarming story *My Daughter, Myself* is a must read and a major contributing factor to such a powerful and healing movement. This beautiful book provides peace and connection to those suffering unimaginable pain.'

James Thomas, *co-founder of Feel the Magic*

'The greatest emotions are soulful and indescribable. In *My Daughter, Myself*, Connie Easterbrook tells grief like it is, from the heart. She gives us a deep and moving insight into the powerful inner life of the bereaved, and the soul's journey through loss. Connie weaves a tapestry that envelops the reader, and brings us an acute observation of how family relationships and the grief journey play out amidst the generational trauma of our family of origin. She also gives us a window into what she describes as "the inner light" of those we have loved and lost – the light we do not always see in its totality when they are alive, "the transcendent power of the invisible string".'

Patricia Therese Benedict Thomas, *Grief Care managing consultant*

'Connie took me on a journey that was not only deeply moving but also inspiring and hopeful. At times I felt as if she was writing directly to me! She shares her story of loss, anguish, pain and self-discovery in a way that is remarkably brave, honest and raw. Throughout the book there are gems of wisdom and advice based on her personal experience as a grieving mother and as a wise and insightful therapist.'

Karen Triggs, *MA Art Therapy, BA Psychology, Grad Dip Sexology, B Teaching*

my daughter, *myself*

A quest towards understanding in the face of loss

CONNIE EASTERBROOK

BOOK THERAPY

Published in 2022 by Book Therapy
booktherapy.com.au

Copyright © Connie Easterbrook 2022

The moral rights of the author have been asserted.

All rights reserved. No part of this book may be reproduced or transmitted in any form or by any means, electronic or mechanical, including photocopying, recording or by any information storage and retrieval system, without prior permission in writing from the publisher. The Australian *Copyright Act 1968* (the Act) allows a maximum of one chapter or 10 per cent of this book, whichever is the greater, to be photocopied by any educational institution for its educational purposes provided that the educational institution (or body that administers it) has given a remuneration notice to the Copyright Agency (Australia) under the Act.

The events, places and conversations in this memoir have been re-created from memory. The chronology of some events has been compressed. When necessary, the names and identifying characteristics of individuals and places have been changed to maintain anonymity.

ISBN: 978-0-6455714-1-7

Cover design by Joanne Buckley
Edited by Alison Fraser
Proofread by Dannielle Viera
Printed by IngramSpark

*For Simone, in remembrance of you
and the light that you brought to life
and all that I have learnt through you,
and from you.*

*For Tony, without whose support
I could not have written this book.*

*And for my amazing children –
Daniel, Laura and Matthew.*

Your children are not your children.
They are the sons and daughters of Life's longing for itself.
They come through you but not from you.
And though they are with you yet they belong not to you.

You may give them your love but not your thoughts,
For they have their own thoughts.
You may house their bodies but not their souls,
For their souls dwell in the house of tomorrow,
which you cannot visit, not even in your dreams.
You may strive to be like them, but seek not to make them like you.
For life goes not backward nor tarries with yesterday.
You are the bows from which your children as living arrows are sent forth.
The archer sees the mark upon the path of the infinite, and
He bends you with His might that His arrows may go swift and far.
Let your bending in the Archer's hand be for gladness;
For even as He loves the arrow that flies,
So He loves also the bow that is stable.

—Kahlil Gibran, *The Prophet*[1]

TABLE OF CONTENTS

FOREWORD		xiii
PROLOGUE		xv
INTRODUCTION		1
CHAPTER 1:	Her Inner Light	3
CHAPTER 2:	Simone	15
CHAPTER 3:	Connie's Story	25
CHAPTER 4:	Simone and Me	41
CHAPTER 5:	Marriage and Children	65
CHAPTER 6:	And Then There Were More	77
CHAPTER 7:	Losing Simone	87
CHAPTER 8:	Grieving Simone	101
CHAPTER 9:	Early Experiences of Grief	107
CHAPTER 10:	The Challenges of Grief	117
CHAPTER 11:	Life is What Happens …	135
CHAPTER 12:	Life After the Loss of My Brother	145
CHAPTER 13:	Losing Mum	153
CHAPTER 14:	Insights About Grief	167
CHAPTER 15:	Ongoing Struggles with Grief	177
CHAPTER 16:	'Getting Over It'	187
CHAPTER 17:	What I Have Learnt About Mental Health	193
	About ADHD	194
	About anger	195
	About anxiety	201

	About depression	203
	About the inner critic	207
	About parenting	212
	The importance of self-care	217
CHAPTER 18:	Drawing the Threads Together	221
APPENDIX A:	Practical Suggestions	228
APPENDIX B:	Mental Health First Aid Skills and Resources	233
ACKNOWLEDGEMENTS		241
RECOMMENDED READING LIST		246
REFERENCES		253

FOREWORD

In over twenty-five years of working in the field of grief and bereavement, I have not come across a book that tells the story of love, loss and how we bear the unbearable with such exquisite honesty, transparency and nuance as *My Daughter, Myself*. Simply stated, it is an extraordinary book. The process of grieving can feel wild, chaotic and unpredictable. Connie Easterbrook takes our hand and walks us through her complex story of loving, losing and reconstructing a world of meaning following the death of her beloved daughter Simone.

For most people, love is the most profound source of pleasure in our lives, while the loss of those we love is the deepest source of pain. Love and loss are two sides of the same coin. We cannot have one without risking the other.

These losses force us to relearn the world and ourselves. Who am I now, in the wake of this seismic loss? Connie explores this question as she explores her identity as a mother, as a community member and in her workplace. These settings can enable or constrain our grief. In addition, how we talk to ourselves about our loss and the compassion we extend to ourselves can help or hinder us as we integrate the lessons of loss.

Grief is idiosyncratic and complex and, although not a toolkit for managing grief, *My Daughter, Myself* contains much wisdom. It examines the importance of rituals, the management of anniversaries, how people engage with loss in myriad ways and how other issues such as complex emotions and mental health can complicate our journey through loss. Importantly, Connie explores how spirituality and being part of a faith community can provide a scaffold of meaning and a community of care and support.

Long-held myths about the grief experience, such as there being a predictable emotional trajectory leading from distress to 'recovery', or that we need to say goodbye to those we love and to 'move on', continue to be held by Western culture. We, in fact, grow around our loss; it never leaves us and whereas death might end a life, it does not end a relationship. Our love is not tied to time or geography.

I hope that this book will be read widely – by those seeking a window into the intense experience of loss as well as those in the helping professions who want to have a deeper insight into the world of grieving people.

This insightful book reminds us that for most of us, the fact that one day we shall lose the ones we love, and they us, draws us closer to them, while bringing awareness of our collective mortality.

***Christopher Hall**, Chief Executive Officer,*
Australian Centre for Grief and Bereavement

PROLOGUE

There are many reasons why I wrote this book. While this is my story about experiences of grief and loss, it is about more than grief alone. And although I tell the story of two lives – of a daughter and her mother – neither does it fit purely within the genre of memoir. My initial intention in writing was to enable Simone to live on in the pages of this book, so that others could come to know her and learn something from the story of her life. And I hoped to give her short life additional meaning and purpose, into the future.

I was also strongly motivated by my desire to share what I have learnt about the joys, trials and complexities of the mother–daughter relationship. I felt that I had something significant to share about the crucial importance of unconditional love and acceptance in assisting us to be the best parent we can be for our children.

As I wrote, unexpectedly, my grief and loss took over. It was as though sorrow took hold of my pen and wrote its own truth. It wasn't planned, it just happened. So, this book has a strong message to share about the raw pain and the struggle of losing someone whom you love. I hope that by reading my words, you will feel less alone and less abnormal throughout your own journey through loss.

I also wanted to share something of my personal journey with mental health struggles, both before and after the loss of my daughter. As I sat and listened, in my capacity as a counsellor, I heard stories from others who struggled with anxiety, depression, low self-esteem and self-worth; they had relationship struggles, they suffered with grief and loss. I was struck by an urgent desire to share my story, especially what I have learnt through my journey, in order to help others, to assist in the process of transforming a life – the way my own life has been transformed.

I felt that I had some insights to share that just might make a difference, and provide encouragement and hope. And if I was able to do it, you might see that you, too, can make it through challenges and emerge stronger and more empowered to make the necessary changes in your life. I wanted you to know that you can find joy, inner peace and healing alongside the grief of losing someone you love, or parenting in a less-than-ideal way, or having been parented imperfectly. You can find self-forgiveness, self-compassion and a new caring, healthy relationship with yourself.

My greatest hope for this book is that it will assist you to build strong, loving relationships with your children. And that you will learn to love and fully accept yourself and grow in grace and self-compassion, as these are the gifts that nurture and develop us as parents and as human beings. I'm hopeful that you will become the best version of yourself, and be able to assist your children to complete this journey for themselves.

INTRODUCTION

My beautiful daughter Simone died in a car accident when she was just twenty-one.

Losing Simone changed me. To lose your child is a heartbreaking, life-changing tragedy. For me, losing Simone was a complicated, heartbreaking, life-changing tragedy.

Simone was my first-born. She was unique – lovable, loving, quirky, joyful, passionate, infuriating, complex, enthusiastic, genuine, frustrating, paradoxical, confusing, amazing! Simone embodied both the best and the worst of me. I loved her, but she frustrated the heck out of me. I spent her entire lifetime trying to be a better mother and, it pains me to admit, trying to make her a better daughter. There were times when our relationship flourished, when we really clicked and could enjoy each other's company. But there were many, many other times when I was not the kind of mother I wanted to be. When I was not the best version of myself.

I have struggled with my own demons – anxiety, depression, anger, low self-esteem, abandonment, guilt, shame, doubting my faith – the whole emotional rollercoaster. And I found parenting hard work.

Significant grief had already been part of my life when Simone died – through the loss of my brother to suicide and my mother to a sudden death by stroke.

I believe that sharing our life stories is a powerful source of learning and that we can heal, grow and transform by understanding how someone else made it through the challenges of their life. I say this because learning from others is what has helped me most. When I hear the stories of friends, clients, writers, teachers, trainers, ministers and colleagues, I learn, I grow, I change. Robert Atkinson[2] reflects that understanding our own life journey assists us to comprehend not only ourselves but also others and the world we live in. He considers the sharing of life stories to be a source of connection between us and a benefit for us all.

What helps me most when I read others' stories is knowing that I am not alone, that others have walked a similar path and they've survived. Others have experienced pain, grief, loss, sadness and heartache and they made it through. And, most importantly – for me, anyway – they didn't make it through easily or perfectly. They made mistakes, failed, stuffed up. It is through their humanity, not through their perfection, that I am encouraged.

Although I work as a qualified counsellor, and will be drawing from psychology and counselling principles and sources as I write, I am speaking foremost from one imperfect human being to another.

I want Simone's life to have made as much difference as it can. I want my own life to make as much difference as it can.

So, this is for you, Simone. And for me. And it's also for you, dear reader …

CHAPTER 1

HER INNER LIGHT

Have you ever known someone whose presence radiated warmth, light and sincerity? Someone who, when you looked into their eyes, beamed out joy, sparking joy. And when you looked closer you noticed that the joy was mixed with love, peace, goodness, warmth, compassion, contentment and hope.

All my life I have been looking out for people like that. Not actively searching for them, just watching and noticing. Wanting to be near them, to live my life with them. They are a blessing to be around. I have been fortunate enough to know some people like that, people whose lives have intersected with mine, sometimes briefly, sometimes longer. Simone had that inner light. It lived and breathed within her.

Although I lived and loved Simone for twenty-one years – somehow, I didn't fully appreciate that light. In our too brief time together, I only recognised glimpses of this light, this beauty of spirit. It was only after she was taken from me that I realised her inner light had been there all the time. I just didn't always see it, or value it. I paid close attention when this light emanated from others, and yet I failed to appreciate it in my own daughter.

Her friends saw it; one of Simone's fellow youth group leaders, Bec, speaking after her death, said of her, 'Your radiant soul shone out of you and lit up any room you entered. You had this joy inside of you that was so intense that it looked like it could just burst out of you.' I couldn't have captured Simone's essence better myself.

Then how could I have been so blind as to not appreciate and enjoy the treasure that I had been living with all those years? After she died, it was as if the scales fell from my eyes and I could finally see her, understand her, appreciate her. But I saw it too late. This is my heartache. To recognise this truth about Simone when I could no longer celebrate, love and enjoy her, completely, unconditionally.

There were times – glimpses – when I experienced her inner light. One such glimpse occurred on our last family day out together, three days before the accident. It was Father's Day, 2008. Tony (my husband) and Simone were keen to go to Cockatoo Island, to view the installation art for the Biennale of Sydney,* so we decided to make it a family occasion.

It was a beautiful day. It was cool, still early spring, but the sky was clear and blue. We sat outside on the ferry for a while, enjoying the sea and being on a boat. Simone was so excited about showing us all the art installations that she had seen on an earlier visit to the island. We retreated after a while into the warmth of the ferry. The interior was old, faded and dilapidated. As we sat there, the conversation turned to eye colour and genetically inherited traits.

---

* The Biennale of Sydney is a non-profit organisation that presents a large exhibition of contemporary visual arts in a festival format. It is held biennially for three months and includes artist talks, forums, guided tours and family days. All are free to the public.

What happened next is crystal clear. It's a moment that has been frozen in time, printed evocatively in my mind's eye. I was sitting down and Simone was standing up, excited and restless, looking around and chattering nonstop, as was her way. Simone was insisting that her eyes were more blue than green. I disagreed, 'No, they are definitely more green than blue.' Then I stopped and looked carefully into her eyes, staring at them for a long, full moment. As I stared, I was captured by the love and warmth in her eyes. I forgot to look at what colour they really were. All I could see was the joy, warmth, wisdom and love staring back at me, through her eyes.

She really loves me, I thought, with surprise.

I have never forgotten that moment. A moment where we connected, mother to daughter. Oh, how often since have I wished that I could stare into her eyes forever.

When Simone died, she was twenty-one. She stood 165 cm tall. She had long, thick, honey blonde hair that she often fiddled with when reflective or distracted. She had greeny-blue eyes that sparkled with interest, honesty and warmth.

If you were new to Simone, you might find her quiet, shy and reserved, maybe a little withdrawn. You might have a hard time making eye contact. Sometimes, she looked a little dazed, as though her mind was caught up in some other place, some other time zone. As she grew up, she had become short-sighted, so she always had to wear glasses. By the age of twenty-one, however, she had graduated to contact lenses, so she wore her glasses less frequently. Her last pair of glasses had a cool red frame that suited her colouring; I thought they made her look quite trendy and interesting.

Simone had a small face, clear pale skin and, quite naturally, the most perfectly shaped and arched eyebrows I have ever seen. She never plucked her eyebrows, they just grew this way. She had small features, with a dainty nose, small ears and mouth. Her face often held a secretive little smile. A Mona Lisa smile. When she was embarrassed, her face would suffuse with colour; it was hard for her to blush discreetly! Her colouring was best suited to bright colours, rather than neutral tones. She looked great in reds, oranges, hot pinks and floral prints; black, too, always looked good on her.

In build, Simone had a petite frame, though with what you might call child-bearing hips and a generous bottom – characteristics that often caused her despair when she was trying to find jeans or a figure-flattering dress. She had long arms, with elegant, long, tapered fingers, perfect for playing the piano or, in her case, holding a paintbrush.

If you met Simone at a social gathering, you would expect to find her in a colourful, feminine dress. Or a pretty skirt and top. If you met her at university, she would probably be wearing her favourite art jeans. They were a casual, comfortable style, ripped in places and spattered with paint remnants, from many happy hours spent painting and creating artworks.

Simone was generally quietly spoken and gentle in nature. She was kind and caring, and had a heart that always wanted to help others – whether it was listening to her siblings and friends when they were going through tough times, knitting a scarf to cheer up a good friend, or her involvement in church, ministering to children and adolescent girls.

Those who knew Simone could not help but be taken in by the joy and radiance that shone from her eyes. It seemed like an aura to me at times, a glow that physically emanated from her radiant expression.

When she looked at me, I often felt that she had a knowing look in her eyes. As though she really got me, genuinely understood me.

Generally, Simone preferred to avoid the spotlight. She was more of a behind-the-scenes kind of girl, working well with a team, but also independently, on whatever her role required. Neither would she be the life of the party – she was more likely to be involved in quiet conversations with others.

Once you got to know Simone, however, you would often find her to be very talkative, excitable and enthusiastic, especially if she was talking about a subject close to her heart – such as her family, art or Christianity. Simone could be intense – she had strong views on a variety of subjects – and as she became more comfortable with you, she would share more of her mind and heart. I wouldn't call her a touchy-feely kind of person, but if she loved you, her hugs were warm and generous.

In the heart of our close-knit, loving family, Simone was affectionate, kind, caring and bubbly. She was a passionate, vibrant girl full of life, love, affection, humour and fun. She talked a lot. She always had a lot to say, to share. She was an interesting companion and observer of life. I knew that I could have a day out with Simone and it would be filled with conversation, fun, good food, multiple cups of tea, intense discussion and strong views on a variety of subjects. She felt things deeply. She had so much personality, so much character, that her influence on each of us remains with us strongly.

Simone filled a unique role. Eldest daughter, eldest sister, upholder of good morals and strong values. She was a central force in our household. Without intending to do so, she embodied the heart and soul of our family. Like most of us, she was most fully herself at home. Although she talked a lot, she also listened when she knew you needed it. Her brothers, Daniel and Matt, sister Laura and her many friends will attest to this. She had lots of interests – art, books, relationships, Christianity, philosophy, politics, history – each of which would preoccupy her at times.

Her mood could change like the wind. It was often hard to know which Simone you were going to get. From excited and passionate, to moody quietness, to sadness, to annoyance and inflexibility. Sometimes to anger, especially first thing in the morning. She was not a morning person! We all remember her resounding thumping up and down the stairs first thing in the morning. None of the younger kids wanted to be the one to wake her up in the morning; they said it was too scary!

Sometimes, Simone could be pretty hyper. This would express itself in loud and enthusiastic renditions of her favourite songs, loud and fervent conversations on topics of interest, or just constant jiggling and movement. If she was really happy and enjoying herself, she was known to literally be swinging and dancing, full of life and energy. My daughter Laura recalls her coming back from the city with the church youth group and swinging around the train poles.

At other times, Simone was the opposite of bubbly. I was surprised to notice that on our home videos Simone often avoided the camera and her presence was quiet and serene. These videos don't show the loud, chatty person I remember her to be.

One of the qualities I valued about Simone was her enthusiasm for life. I loved how excited she became about the matters that interested her. When Simone was into something, she was fully into it. No half measures. This did lead, however, to some full-on experiences. If Simone liked somebody, she loved them – she was consumed by her interest in them. (I am thinking romantic relationships here.) She was also a devoted and loyal friend, not giving up on people easily.

She loved the Harry Potter series of books, reading and re-reading them multiple times, and was heavily into fan fiction, even writing her own version of wizarding stories. If she was reading a book, often a thick fantasy novel, she was fully engrossed within its pages and found it hard to pull herself away, back to real life. She often loved to quote and perform lines from her favourite movies. She watched some of these movies so often she could quote infinite lines of script. She loved comedies – the Monty Python movies and *Robin Hood: Men in Tights* – especially romantic comedies. Some of her favourites were *Ever After: A Cinderella Story*, *50 First Dates* and *Never Been Kissed* to name a few. Simone had a zany sense of humour, but it was never at another's expense.

She also loved to play on the computer – sometimes too much – at the expense of her university studies or sleeping time. She became obsessed with the Sims game, devoting countless hours to developing a virtual Easterbrook family, focusing on making sure this computer-generated family matched our own real family as closely as possible.

Simone's tendency to be fully into everything she did often led to her running late. She was the one who drove the kids to youth group, and sometimes to school or on other excursions, but she couldn't be trusted to be on time. A common sight was Simone finishing off a talk or study to present at youth group – still writing it – as she was walking out the door! Or printing if off at the very last minute. This also happened with school and university assignments, projects or artworks.

Simone tended to travel heavy. If she was going away for a holiday, even a camping trip, she would spend many happy hours selecting a wide range of clothes and accessories to bring along. Simone was renowned for this in her church group and Beach Mission; it was expected that she would be accompanied by large bags of clothes, and also a multitude of art supplies and craft resources to share.

Simone loved to eat. She had a particular love of lollies, ice-cream, raw cake or cookie mixture, bacon and meat, any kind of meat. She was quite the carnivore! Simone was never interested in alcohol, but she adored tea. She was one of the early converts to T2, before they became popular. At her instigation, we put up a cupboard in our kitchen dedicated to all things tea – a multitude of different flavours and types of tea, as well as teapots, tea caddies and teacups. This love of hers was definitely passed on to the rest of our family.

She often had cold hands. She suffered from poor circulation and developed juvenile arthritis, which was quite painful. So, she was often warmly dressed, complete with gloves and beanie. She had a pink beanie that she loved to wear, and she definitely preferred the heat to the cold.

Daniel, Laura and Matt remember Simone as being very motherly in nature, calling her their second mum. When I wasn't very patient or calm brushing Laura's hair, she turned to her sister for help. When she got her period, she put some of her awkward and confused questions to Simone. When Daniel or Laura felt isolated in social situations, they would seek Simone out so they didn't feel so alone. When I was busy or preoccupied, they would turn to Simone for comfort or help.

Tony enjoyed having robust conversations with Simone, often late at night or when they were travelling together. He enjoyed her interest in a wide variety of subjects and found her to be like a sponge, eager to soak up knowledge and information. He enjoyed going out with her to art exhibitions, galleries or installations. They had a shared interest in modern art, so they loved hanging out at the Museum of Contemporary Art as well as the Art Gallery of NSW.

Simone had an enormous sense of self-confidence and self-belief. If she set her mind to do something, nothing would hold her back. She didn't seem to worry about what other people thought of her – a quality I must admit that I envied. She would walk around the university campus laden with multiple huge canvases, with no thought of how she might appear to others. If Simone wanted to do something, such as the Duke of Edinburgh scheme, she would do it; she wouldn't be held back if none of her friends wanted to join. She wore her painting jeans with pride. She talked about her Christian faith blatantly and brazenly; she was never apologetic or reserved about her beliefs. Her Facebook page featured a bold statement of her Christian beliefs. She drove the family van – a Nissan Nomad people mover – with pride, filled to the seams with canvases and art paraphernalia, blaring Christian rock music, loud and strong. You could hear Simone coming down our street before you saw her car!

Simone was a curious mixture of contradictions. Though there were many areas in her life where she aimed for perfection – the utmost that she could achieve – there were others where she didn't seem to care at all. She dressed carefully and was particular about her physical appearance, and she also dressed to make a statement – such as her infamous jeans, covered with rips and paint. When it came to the finer details of life, everything had to be perfect. For instance, it could take Simone up to ten minutes to make a sandwich. Everything had to be cut perfectly to size; there needed to be a variety of colours and textures. She approached sandwich-making as though she was creating a work of art, and this held true in other areas, too.

Yet her personal habits tended towards messiness, untidiness and disorganisation. Wherever Simone went, she left a trail. I often joked that I could tell where she had been by the clues left behind – chocolate and lolly wrappers tucked into the side of the lounge, curtains haphazardly half-open/half-closed (to hide the fact that she had been watching movies half the day), cupboard doors and drawers left open. Her bedroom was disorganised – clothes strewn over the floor, remnants of leftover food and drinks perched precariously, multiple books and myriad different papers and drawings piled high.

Simone was at her happiest when she was involved in some form of art or craft, whether this was in her bedroom, or using the garage as an art room or out in the world. She loved to bring her pencils and paintbrushes to the beach or into the bush, either alone, with her friends or with her sister Laura. She was also passionate about sharing her art and craft skills with the community, either at church or other local events. She was active in the children's ministries at church and she supported them diligently. These were activities such as Q-club, Beach Mission, Girls' Brigade, fetes and outreach. She would paint faces, paint banners and do myriad amazing crafts: using all her artistic gifts and skills to inspire and entertain kids.

Another important aspect of Simone's character was her willingness to engage in deep philosophical discussions, mostly about God and the meaning of life, but also about other intellectual concepts, such as history, politics and art. She discussed these matters late into the night with her dad, her brother Daniel, other close friends and me.

Simone was a person who held very high moral and ethical values and standards. She had strong personal beliefs about living a godly and obedient life, and about obeying the letter of the law. Simone would never speed or ever deliberately break any road rule.

I have some special memories of Simone that I will always treasure. One of these was when we ran the church bookshop together. Every six weeks, we would restock the collection at the WORD Bookstore at Dee Why. This was an all-day affair, requiring a long car journey, the choosing of books and, if we could fit both in, morning tea and lunch. I loved this time we shared together. We used to talk nonstop, all the way there and back. It was a special bonding time for us because we both loved books. It was good to get away from the stresses of home and do something we enjoyed together.

I also cherish the times we spent shopping together. We both loved buying clothes, shoes and cosmetics – girly things. One of our favourite places to shop was Target, where we would spend many happy hours trying things on, discussing the merits of outfits and checking each other's choices. The change-room lady got to know us so well that she would greet us by name and with a welcoming smile at each visit!

Simone was at her happiest when our family was all out together. When we were all on a family outing, Simone beamed – that's the only description for it. Her friends also attest to this quality about her, telling me that Simone often spoke about her brothers and sister, and this continued through youth group and at university.

I think that the most important legacy Simone gave, especially to her siblings, was being an amazing spiritual role model. Simone's faith in God was evident in everything she did; she not only talked about it all the time, but also lived it every day. People have made positive comments to me about my family, and I give a lot of the credit to Simone. She was such a good role model – she exemplified many of the positive attributes that parents want their children to reflect and achieve. Yet the one quality that shines out above all the others, and this has been borne out through discussions with Simone's friends and her church family, is Simone's inspiring faith in God.

Simone's faith really defined who she was as a person. Simone's passion was God – service to God and telling others about God, to bring them to personal salvation. I cannot think of Simone without reflecting that she was, truly, one of God's great ambassadors. I hope this chapter has begun to paint a portrait of the Simone we knew and loved, and you have some sense of the strong, amazing young woman she was.

CHAPTER 2

SIMONE

Simone Maree Easterbrook was born on St Patrick's Day, the seventeenth of March, in 1987. It was a special and significant day for our family. It was special for Tony and me because it was the birth of our first child. It was significant for our families because Simone was the first grandchild on both sides. There was a lot of excitement and joy, as both families rushed to visit at the hospital where she was born.

It was also a significant date because it was the anniversary of my maternal grandparents' wedding. Later, sadly, it was the date of my husband's maternal grandmother's passing. It was also a symbolic and distinctive day in another way.

The seventeenth of March has been made famous by the patron of the Irish, St Patrick. It's not, as you might anticipate, a celebration of his birth, but of his death in AD 461. As I reflect upon Simone's life and who she was as a person, she shared some characteristics that mirror the special day on which she was born. St Patrick's life was originally celebrated because of his passionate zeal to convert the Irish to Christianity. In today's world, it has become the day to commemorate and celebrate the unique and quirky aspects of all things Irish.

Passionate, unique and quirky. These are just three words among many that describe Simone. She was passionate about her Christian faith and demonstrated evangelistic zeal throughout her young life. She was also unique and quirky, not in an Irish sense, but in what I can only describe as a Simone sense. She was one of a kind – not only to those who knew and loved her, but even to those who only knew her briefly. I guess most parents think that their child is special: unique and unlike any other child on Earth. As indeed, they are. But there was something about Simone …

When Simone was born, she was so quiet and peaceful. Serene. She hardly gave a cry as she was brought into the world. I remember looking into her face and her expression was curiously vague. It seemed to be saying, 'What's all the fuss about?' As a baby, Simone was quiet, placid and often serious. We had to work hard to even raise a smile. Both my mum and my mother-in-law used to say that she was 'an old soul', one who has been here many times before. I didn't know. She was my first baby and, not having had extended family around as I was growing up, I had no idea of what was normal. As the first grandchild, Simone was lavished with love and attention by her proud grandparents, and her aunts and uncles.

Around the time of Simone's first birthday, her personality started to emerge. She became active, curious and adventurous. Her quirky sense of humour had already begun to develop, and the strangest things would make her smile and laugh. Simone was, as I've said, a curious mixture. She could be really out there – laughing, chattering, showing off. But at other times she was very quiet, withdrawn into her own little world.

As a young child, she had boundless energy and found it very hard to sit still. She was constantly moving, fidgeting and restless. To sit still in a chair in an upright position was an impossible chore for Simone.

Mealtimes could be quite chaotic, because she would suddenly want to get up and investigate, or come round to you and give you a big hug and kiss. At around the age of three or four, Simone could be shy and not say a word around people she knew, but bound up to strangers and start telling them her life story.

Daniel came along when Simone was three, and I needed time to feed and take care of him. In order to keep Simone quiet and settled, I would often sit her down with paper, crayons and pencils, and she would draw for hours on end. From the time that Simone was five or six, a prolific outpouring of drawings and paintings began – never colouring-in books, as these were not creative enough for Simone. When she was about eight, she had a passion for Ariel, the Disney mermaid. Hundreds of pictures of this little mermaid were drawn – I guess she was perfecting her skills.

Simone's primary-school teachers loved her, on the whole. She was one of those children that adults think are cute, but other kids see as 'different'. Kids, even in kindergarten and primary school, seem to have a radar to detect kids who don't fit the norm. And Simone was unique. Simone was always herself; she was her own person, and was never influenced by what the crowd said and did. As a mother, I worried about these differences: I wanted her to fit in.

Simone often came across as awkward or a little clumsy. She would talk too much at times; yet at other times, when she needed to talk, she didn't. And she was impulsive, blurting information out at inopportune times. She also had a hard time sitting still on her classroom chair, a quality that not all her teachers tolerated.

She was also unpredictable at primary-school age. I never knew what she would decide to do next. For example, I would advise her to stay within the school gates if I was late for school pick-up or, if she felt concerned, to go to the front office. But I couldn't count on her doing this. Sometimes she would wander to our friend's house up the street and, other times, she would go back into the schoolyard and play, out of sight. At times, it seemed like Simone was in another time zone. She was dreamy and vague, what some people might call a space cadet.

I wondered about these qualities: her restlessness and high energy levels; her difficulties in listening and paying attention. Getting Simone ready for school was an exercise in patience. She took so long to get dressed and ready, to eat breakfast, and I always had to repeat myself about tasks that needed to be done. I put these qualities down to normal childhood behaviour, something that she would grow out of. However, when Simone was about seven or eight, I picked up a book in a library that talked about attention deficit hyperactivity disorder (ADHD). I read the list of symptoms and was shocked to realise that Simone fit every single one of them, about twelve or thirteen in all. Could this be the answer?

I made an appointment with a paediatrician, who administered a range of questionnaires to fill in, by us, her parents, and also by teachers at her school. The results confirmed that Simone had ADHD, combined type.* This diagnosis, though confronting and disturbing, did bring some clarity and understanding about why Simone was the way she was. Simone's experiences of ADHD affected her life, and mine, in many ways.

When Simone wasn't drawing, she was restless. As she matured, this restlessness played out in constantly needing stimulation, and in using more than one sense at any one time. It wasn't enough for

---

* ADHD has been subdivided into three forms: predominantly hyperactive/impulsive, predominantly inattentive and combined type, which is a mixture of hyperactive/impulsive and inattentive.

Simone to just watch television or a movie, to simply sit through a lecture or a church service – she had to be doing something with her hands as well: doodling, drawing, knitting or fiddling with her hair. Simone told me that she could concentrate better when she had a few things happening at once because it enabled her to focus better.

Simone continued to be different when she went to high school. And high-school kids don't like difference either. While Simone made some friends at school, she did experience bullying. When she was in years 7 and 8, the school counsellor rang to say they were concerned about her quietness and tendency to keep to herself. When we spoke to Simone about this, she spoke of some nasty behaviour by groups of boys and girls. The school had a great welfare program in place, so they did what they could to support her. But, as a mother, I worried. I never stopped worrying, actually. Anxiety about Simone was my constant companion throughout her life.

Although outwardly quiet and shy to many, and suffering from anxiety in social situations, at home she was the opposite. Bubbly and effervescent, constantly talking, always affectionate and loving, full of personality and life. I often wished that others could see this side of Simone. Although shy, Simone pushed at her own constraints – involving herself in activities that more confident people would find challenging. She would attend Girls' Brigade camps and youth group camps, and her determination led her to achieve a Bronze Duke of Edinburgh Award, despite not having a close friend alongside her. I really admired this tenacity in Simone.

One of the attributes that I prized most about Simone was her love and commitment to her brothers and sister. When I was about to give birth to her brother Daniel, I was warned to expect jealousy, tantrums and bad behaviour, in response to having a sibling to compete with.

This never happened. Simone adored her brother. She played with him patiently for hours during his baby and toddler years. As they grew up, they spent a lot of their time together, initially playing in the bush around our home, or playing board and computer games, enjoying movies and television together. Later, this extended into going to church together, and having heart-to-heart discussions. They were best friends.

Similarly, when Laura was born five years later, Simone was a reliable source of help, often holding, feeding or caring for Laura when I was busy. And as Laura grew up, Simone was a consistent friend to her. They enjoyed painting together, and Simone also fostered her spiritual development, leading Laura to make her own commitment to God when she was just eight years old. Four years later, when Matthew arrived to complete our family, Simone continued to be a source of support for me, and a good playmate and friend to her siblings.

Another highlight from Simone's early years, which continued throughout her life, was her love of dressing up. As a young child, she loved to dress up with her siblings and friends. Her brother Daniel, as a preschooler, was often dressed up by Simone. And the desire to dress up never stopped for Simone. If there was a party, it had to be dress-up. Church dress-ups and holiday Bible clubs were another opportunity to be creative and dress up. Consequently, Simone's eighteenth birthday had the theme of 'Formal or Foolish'. Simone wore her elegant black formal dress, complete with tiara.

Everything that Simone achieved had to be perfect, original and big. The amount of planning and preparation Simone put into her twenty-first birthday party was staggering. The theme was 'ancient times', as in, she was ancient because she was turning twenty-one! Simone researched different ancient foods of the world and wanted us to prepare at least one dish from every ancient cuisine. The scene had to be just right, with attention to all the decorating details, and Simone dressed up Japanese-style, complete with a black wig and kimono. It came together in the end, with all the family pitching in to help, and Simone was really happy with how her party turned out. She had so much enthusiasm, commitment and passion, and I loved that about her.

During her life, Simone continued to develop an interest and proficiency in drawing, craft and art. She went to after-school art classes and studied visual arts and design and technology in years 9–12. At both primary and high school, Simone received many awards for her artworks and studies in visual arts, achieving the school medal for the highest visual arts result in the Higher School Certificate (HSC). She was also selected to attend the prestigious National Art School's life-drawing classes, as an extra elective for her HSC, and she excelled at it, after she got over her embarrassment at the nude models!

Simone's final HSC projects are a testament to her hard work, imagination and determination. For design and technology, she developed a 'Roll-a-Reader' – an illuminated scroll, complete with a detailed portfolio, prepared with the help of Tony (for his technical skills), me (for editorial assistance) and her aunty Jane (for word-processing skills). Her major work for visual arts was an exhibition of twenty exquisite portraits, presented in a wide variety of mediums (crayons, chalk, paint, ink and pencil). It was chosen to be exhibited in the *Art Rules* exhibition at the local art gallery in Gymea.

Drawing and painting were full-time pursuits for Simone; she was happiest spending much of her free time doing some form of art or craft. Even though she went on to complete a Bachelor of Creative Arts and a Graduate Diploma in Education, university assignments were a huge challenge. It was hard for Simone to condense all her information into the required word count – 1,000 or 2,000 words were never enough for all she had to say. I was her editor-in-chief, which took up many of my hours. This was a challenging and stressful time for me. I worked part-time, studied part-time and I had four children. Life was busy, very busy. But my first priority was to be there for my children, and I really wanted Simone to succeed in her chosen field of study. It wasn't unusual for me to spend late nights, and chunks of time on the weekend, helping her to organise and edit her assignments.

Simone's final artwork for her Bachelor of Creative Arts at the University of Wollongong showcased her enthusiasm and passion (and her usual tendency to overdo things). While most students painted one or two pictures, Simone executed five massive paintings, with an additional fifteen drawings and other artworks in various mediums of a scene at Deadman's Creek on Heathcote Road. All were created onsite because she believed that a true artist needed to have a sense of the site to produce their best work.

After completing her undergraduate degree, Simone decided to combine her love of art with her passion for working with children. We agreed that this would be the perfect match for Simone's skills and experience. So, in the following year, Simone began studies for a Graduate Diploma in Education, also at the University of Wollongong. However, the course was very demanding. It was the first year when a two-year course was condensed into one year. After a mere three weeks of study, students were dropped in the deep end and had their first student placement, at a high school. Simone's placement was in the south-western suburbs of Sydney, with a difficult school population. It was a baptism of fire, which required organisation, planning and foresight, not Simone's greatest strengths. It was tough – very tough – but Simone persevered, the way she did with most things. And while she received mixed results and responses to her student placements and studies, she was integrating her learning, and her tutors were confident that she would emerge as a teacher by the end of the year.

Simone was in the springtime of her life. She had recently matured and blossomed into a beautiful young woman. In my mind, I poetically link her to a pure white rose. As we witnessed her developing maturity, we held high hopes for the inspiring teacher and the wonderful wife and mother she would become.

When Simone died, she was a few short weeks away from graduating, and was completing her final practical teaching placement. Simone had a genuine zeal for helping children, and was particularly drawn to those who were struggling with life and learning. I believe that not only would her students have flourished in their creative skills, but they would have felt cared for and validated by Simone's belief in them. We saw this when she did her practical teaching sessions, both from what she told us and also from feedback from her mentoring teachers. We had already witnessed it with Simone's work with the kids in church ministry, whether locally or at Beach Mission; even as far north as the Mid North Coast when she ministered to young First Nations children.

I have shared this account of Simone in the hope that she may inspire, challenge and teach you and others, through the story of her life. Although her time here was short, she made a significant impact on the many people whose lives intersected with hers. This was especially true in relation to her family and friends, but also those with whom she shared her skills and gifts. Many benefited from the warmth of her care for them, from her passion for life and for God, and from her artistic flair and artworks. I hope I have demonstrated that even if you may struggle to be accepted by your peers, or experience the challenge of having a brain that is wired atypically, that you, too, can make a difference in the world through your life.

CHAPTER 3

CONNIE'S STORY

It isn't easy to be vulnerable, to candidly shine a light on the reality of your own life. I am taking comfort and impetus from the words of writers such as Brené Brown[3] and Glennon Doyle,[4] to name two who have authentically and courageously opened up about their life experiences. So, I share with honesty, hoping that the mistakes I've made encourage you through your own imperfect journey.

My relationship with Simone has shaped much of my adult life. When I look back over my life, with particular focus on my inner life – my emotional, intellectual and spiritual journey – I become aware of just how much of my life has been impacted by my experiences of life with Simone.

Many writers have attempted to capture the mother–daughter relationship, which is so often complex and multifaceted. For me, it was precious, delightful and loving, but also difficult and challenging. I never felt as if I got our relationship right; it never felt easy or natural. I felt as though I failed at mothering her, at mothering her in a way I could stand by, proud and strong. In order for you to understand the reasons more deeply, I think it would be helpful for me to share my own life journey. Because the story of mothering Simone is, inextricably, also the story of me. The experiences of my life provide the context and the background from which my relationship with Simone was formed. To understand why I struggled with her, I have had to delve into my own life experiences.

Reflection and self-awareness are crucial tools in understanding ourselves and our close relationships, as are a consideration of family patterns. Understanding our own life story and the relationship we have with our mother, and they with theirs, helps to make sense of the way we think, feel and behave. Unfortunately, I am unable to make reference to my mother's experiences of mothering me. She is no longer with us to tell her part of the story, so that element is incomplete, but I do know that we are all interconnected – my daughter, my mother, myself. Like all of us are, in the circle of life.

I am the eldest daughter of Dutch immigrant parents. They came to Australia as part of the wave of assisted immigration in the 1950s. My dad Joe (short for Johannes) came to seek employment and a brighter future; my mum Will (short for Willempje) followed him eighteen months later, with her wedding dress packed in her luggage. Mum and Dad were the only ones in their respective families to immigrate, so they were very much alone here, apart from two of my dad's friends, who also immigrated. My mum was the second youngest child of a family of ten, and my dad is a middle son, from a family of six, so there is a huge family network in Holland; but, for most of our lives, we have been without any wider family to support our immediate family. It has certainly made us a very tight-knit group.

I had two younger brothers: John, who is three years younger, and Danny, eight years younger. I was the leader of all our childhood adventures, and we had lots of fun together. We climbed trees, caught tadpoles in the local creek, made homemade billycarts and delighted in racing down the biggest hills we could find; we made cubbyhouses in our backyard willow tree and, for a real treat, went to the local sandhills (at Kurnell, now long gone) for fun careening down the slopes. Yes, I was a bit of a tomboy back then!

I loved both my brothers fiercely, and thought of my youngest brother Danny as my child. I loved to mother him. When I got over my disappointment that he wasn't a girl, our relationship flourished. I was his champion if he was in trouble, always ready to defend and explain away any errant behaviour.

We were a Christian family, and I attended the local Methodist church, beginning with Sunday school and going all the way through to youth group. I remember loving to dress in my Sunday best and I would march my brothers proudly up the street to our church. I would often read to my brothers and encourage their faith, as they grew older. When Danny was about nine or ten, I helped him make his own personal commitment to God, which is a treasured memory of mine.

Growing up, I always felt that my family was pretty normal on the whole, although 'normal' is a highly debatable term, really. We spent a lot of time with predominantly Dutch friends, whom Mum and Dad knew through their involvement in the Dutch church and community. I often feel nostalgic when I hear Dutch accents, smell good strong coffee or enjoy iconic Dutch treats, such as speculaas biscuits, beef croquettes or almond pastries: all bring back poignant memories of my childhood.

It wasn't until I was involved with my husband's family that I realised how strongly my life had been impacted by growing up within a Dutch family. I call it the 'Dutch factor' now, and have observed many similarities in people who have been raised in Dutch households. The Dutch are a tough people. *Sterkte*, meaning strength, is the chief value they live by. All those centuries of fighting the sea, of taking and building land from the sea, of building dykes, of fighting foreign invaders by land and sea, have gone into making the Dutch a strong and proud race. They value courage, independence and inner strength. And stoicism. Whenever anything difficult happens in life, all the Dutch people I know say, '*Sterkte*,' which I take to mean, 'Be strong, be tough, you *will* survive this.'

I was always very close to my mother. I talked to her a lot as I was growing up. I always wanted her to listen to my stories, and to hear her perspective on the problems that I wrestled with at school. I needed her affirmation and her praise, which was difficult for Mum, because she struggled with demonstrating her emotions. I never knew if that was just the Dutch factor or something particular about my mother's personality and her way of being in the world. I do remember always needing more from her emotionally than she seemed able to give.

When I started school, it was the first time I had left my mother, as I hadn't attended preschool, and I suffered quite severe separation anxiety. According to my mum's stories, I didn't cope well with school at all; it took many months before she could leave me at school without enduring an emotional scene.

I hated primary school. I was that kid who sat by herself, looking wistful, eating her lunch alone under the shade of a large, leafy gum tree. I probably looked quiet and calm but, on the inside, I was a scared and lonely kid. I remember being afraid of the spiky caterpillars that lurked under the cold metal benches, because I had been pricked by them a few times when my hands went wandering.

During my first couple of years, I made a few friends, but some left the school early because their parents moved out of the area, and others moved on to other friendship groups. When I look back at school photos of myself, I see the reflection of an awkward girl, peering out sadly at the world. In other photos, I am gazing out in a friendly, open manner but, to my eyes, there is something odd about me.

Year 3 (when I was eight) was a big year for me. Our family lived in Holland for three months. I loved it. I met my cousins, had lots of aunts and uncles plying me with love and attention, and had lots of new experiences. Apparently, I learnt the Dutch language quickly and got on well with the family. I felt pretty special going to live in Holland. Like a bit of a celebrity, I had lots of stories to tell on my return.

Unbeknown to me, however, my mother had major health issues and on our flight home she became very ill (she was coughing up blood) and had to be rushed to hospital directly from the airport. She needed to have life-threatening surgery, I know now. It must have been a terrifying time for my parents. As children, we weren't told much, but I'm pretty sure that I absorbed a lot of the fear and anxiety from this time, especially because I was a sensitive child.

My mum suffered from bronchiectasis (a severe lung disease) and the operation to save her life involved removing the diseased part of both her lungs. This was major surgery, and it left behind massive scars that caused a lot of muscular and rheumatic pain for her in later years.

Dad took us to Prince Henry Hospital a few times to visit my mum; it was a frightening experience. It was a scary place that seemed like a gaol to me, with its metal bars over the windows and its isolated location, perched on the edge of a cliff. In order to prevent infection, the beds were positioned two or three metres apart. This made it look even more like a gaol, as if solitary confinement were a punishment for being sick. I have never forgotten the ghastly combination of strong chemical smells while walking along cold, dim corridors, on the trail to find Mum. When we finally found her, she hardly looked or felt like Mum at all. She was connected to all kinds of tubes and equipment, and she appeared very small, pale and sick. Until I gave birth in hospital, which was a happy and positive experience, I always associated hospitals with fear. Even now, the smell of antiseptic causes a cold, sick reverberation in my gut.

In order to recover from the surgery, Mum needed bed rest for three months. Dad needed to return to work and Mum was not able to look after us. So, we were separated, each child farmed out to different family friends while she recovered. I was sent to live with a family five minutes down the road from home, whom I did not know. Apparently, these people were chosen because they lived close to my primary school, which was probably in my best interests, at the time. But I was traumatised by this period among total strangers. The mother was a large Dutch woman with a loud, overpowering personality, who shouted a lot at her three adult children. I remember feeling unsettled and scared.

As a child who continued to struggle with separation anxiety – I have memories of being very upset if I came home to find my mum not there – this was a tough time, which would have felt like abandonment for my eight-year-old self. Research on attachment has verified the traumatic impact of separation from caretakers when a child or parent is in hospital for a lengthy period of time.[5]

Once Mum had been released from hospital (now confined to bed rest), I would often drop in to visit her, as I passed my house on the way to my temporary caretakers. I have one strong memory from this time. On the way to see Mum, I stopped at the local corner store and bought one of those small, white paper bags of mixed lollies, a rare treat. However, the money I had spent (I think it was about ten or twenty cents) was change from my lunch order, which I was meant to return to Mum. I remember my heart beating fast as I walked down the driveway to our back door. I felt so guilty and ashamed about spending this money that I hid the lollies in the bushes alongside our driveway. I went in to see Mum, who was resting in bed, promptly burst into tears and admitted my guilty crime. Mum was horrified by my reaction (not my crime), shocked by how scared I was of her anticipated response. I remember her expressing this to me, which made me feel as though I had failed on two counts. Thinking back on this now, I perceive it to be a reflection of the strong values of honesty, of right and wrong, that had been firmly instilled in me from an early age.

Due to my early struggles to make and keep friends, I thought there was something wrong with me. I remember telling stories, or sharing a doll, trying to do something that would make me appear more special and important, to be more interesting and appealing to others. But it didn't seem to work. I was excluded from the 'in group' at school because, I was told, I wasn't cool enough.

In year 4, when I would have been about nine, I remember an incident that happened in the back courtyard of our primary school. It was morning recess time, and I was just about to go into the library, one of my favourite places to hang out. My two friends came up to me and said, 'Hey, Connie, we are going to join up with Tracey's group from now on. We are so excited, they are really cool, and they said that was all good, but you can't join us. They will only let me and Jenny in. So, we won't be hanging around you anymore.'

I can still remember the shock I felt at the time. I just stared at them, unable to take in this blow to my heart. I felt like crying, but didn't dare to show my feelings. Instead, I looked around at the tall gum trees, feeling isolated and lonely. It is my earliest memory of not feeling good enough.

I never understood why I didn't fit in. In my child's heart, I thought it was due to the way I looked. If only I were prettier, then people would want to be my friend. I never felt good enough 'in my own skin', a sentiment expressed by Leigh Van Der Horst in *Without My Mum*.[6]

I had a number of bullying experiences, too. Some of this related to my christened Dutch name. Although I wasn't known by it casually, it was noted on my birth certificate and was therefore used at school and on other official documentation. My parents had blessed me with the name of Hillagonda Johanna. Talk about an encumbrance, especially when my surname was Hamerslag. Imagine having that called out at roll call! You can imagine the nicknames – Anaconda and Slaggy, to name just a couple. This name had been given to respect both my grandmothers and my Dutch heritage, but was far too woggy for the Australian schoolyard. I found it extremely embarrassing, to the point that I felt ashamed of my identity. My parents didn't appreciate my complaints or my requests to change my name on my birth certificate. They were horrified that I would want to do that.

I was also bullied by some particularly nasty girls, who wrote mean lying letters about me that were distributed behind my back. These experiences left some painful scars. It was like I had an invisible sign on my forehead saying 'PREY'.

There were additional problems at school caused by a lack of coordination and sporting skills. I was always *that* girl, the one who was last to be chosen for any sporting team. I hated that as much as I hated sports, because I wasn't good at anything requiring hand-eye coordination. It reached the point that if I wanted to get out of something I didn't like or wasn't good at, including physical education (PE), sport afternoons, athletic and swimming carnivals, I would start to become ill.

And, most of the time, I genuinely did feel sick. Sick with anxiety, I realise now. So, I had a lot of sick days. Due to my mother's own experience of sickness, she was always more empathic and caring when I wasn't well. I think that was another drawcard to being sick – I received more attention from Mum. I would be tucked into bed and brought nice food, I would watch the midday soaps with Mum and discuss them intensely. This pattern continued into my high-school days, though with less frequency.

In temperament, I was a sensitive child. I was easily overwhelmed and disturbed by how I was feeling on the inside *and* what was happening in the world around me. I struggled with new experiences and situations, I was easily frightened by loud noises, scary television shows and any kind of perceived danger. I was particular about what I ate – if I didn't like the texture, taste or flavour, I wouldn't eat it. I was sensitive to harsh fabrics and textures, and couldn't tolerate wearing clothes that didn't feel comfortable. I remember being forced by Mum to wear a stiff homemade linen dress with navy polka dots, which had a high neckline that was rough on the tender skin around my throat and neck. I thought the dress was ugly and I hated the feel of it. Mum also insisted on a navy parka that I thought was ugly and old – Mum didn't care about that, she just wanted me to be warm. These issues must have been a strain on my mother's patience and tolerance. I realised later, through my studies in counselling and therapy, that I am a highly sensitive person (HSP). This is a trait that has been identified by psychologist Elaine N. Aron, in her book of the same name.[7]

People who are a HSP have heightened levels of sensitivity, including a nervous system that is reactive to both internal and external experiences; this leads to them becoming overwhelmed more easily. Dorothy Corkville Briggs, psychologist and author of *Your Child's Self-Esteem*, corroborates this. Her book discusses the way that some children, genetically, have a nervous system that makes them more sensitive to sensory input. This includes intensities of sound, qualities of light and colour, the textures of different foods and even emotional variations, such as a tone of disapproval or approval.[8]

High school was better than primary. I started to make more friends and, because I was achieving academically, I started to feel better about myself. But I worked very hard to get there. I studied hard from the time I came home till bedtime, every night. I developed my identity and sense of self by being a good student. Looking back, it was almost to the point of an obsession. My projects, assignments and essays were always overdone – if one project book was required, I would fill two. I would spend days or weeks writing major essays and papers. I decorated my books with illustrations or artwork. My printing was so neat, that I was known as The Typewriter. Everything had to be done at the highest standard that I could achieve.

I think that my propensity to overachievement stemmed from a desire to impress others – most importantly, my parents (and in particular, my mum). I remember needing Mum to be proud of my achievements. But I also wanted to know that I could achieve good results for myself; I needed to prove to myself that I was good enough. Although I have now learnt that good enough is never good enough and the pursuit of perfection is a never-fulfilling-enough journey, I did not know this back then.

Mum's ill health continued to have a significant impact on our family. For the remainder of Mum's life, she struggled with chronic ill health. If any viruses or infections were circulating, Mum would catch them. Her immune system was not strong enough to fight them off. She was continually taking antibiotics and/or requiring stronger medication for efficacy. Twice a day, she would lie on a bed with her body and legs raised, in order to drain fluid away from her lungs. Dad made special blocks of wood to raise the bed, and she would lie there and cough up phlegm. This was a normal part of our home life. I didn't think it was strange until I visited friends' homes and realised it was not a normal part of life. I have vivid memories of talking to Mum in the afternoon as she lay there coughing, because she used the bed in my room. Strangely enough, when I look back, I can never see myself in the picture. All I see is Mum – my focus was entirely on her.

When Mum was sick, I felt insecure, unsafe. All my security was bound up with my connection with my mother. While my dad was supportive, during these times he was naturally very busy and stressed, trying to manage working six days per week and caring for my mother, and I don't think he had the time, awareness or ability to give me what I needed. I do remember my father telling me that I talked too much. He had worked hard all day in a noisy factory and, presumably, felt he needed peace and quiet at the dinner table. Yet this led me to feel as though he didn't care about me and my daily experiences. I never seemed to get the responses I needed from my mother either. Somehow, I needed more than she was able to give me.

I now realise that Mum's focus on her ill health meant that she was quite inward-focused. Maybe this is an inevitable part of living with a chronic illness. It also caused my focus to be directed at Mum, leading me to feel invisible and unacknowledged. My petty experiences of bullying and not fitting in didn't seem important in comparison to Mum's issues. In my early high-school years, I wrote an article about Mum for a newspaper competition, talking about your hero. I wrote about how proud I was of my mother – of her resilience in the face of illness, made more difficult because she didn't have family around to support her. Yes, I had put Mum on a very high pedestal and, where there are high expectations, there will inevitably also be a fall from grace.

Mum and I had a close relationship, but we also had our struggles. As a teenager, I felt as though I never lived up to her expectations. I was often in trouble for not helping enough around the house, and being too absorbed in either my schoolwork or my friends. She often said to me how surprised her friends were that I didn't help her more with the housework. This made me feel guilty and ashamed; I didn't like people thinking badly of me. I have realised, in retrospect, that Mum had extremely high expectations for my behaviour, and I never felt as though I reached the mark (I'm not sure anyone could have reached it, certainly not a teenager). Even when I left home, I was admonished for not keeping in touch enough – of thinking more about my friends than I did about her.

When I reached my mid-teens, I became aware that I had a problem with guilt and shame. My mind was constantly harassing me about how bad I was, how I didn't measure up, that I was a bad person. So, what were my perceived sins? Mostly, I considered my thoughts to be atrocious. Whenever I had a negative or judgemental thought – about anyone or anything – I would condemn myself. At times, I felt very angry and frustrated, and I wanted to swear and curse. I would shut the door of my bedroom and shout and bang the furniture around. I never felt able to express my anger in front of my family; it had to be in the privacy of my bedroom. This form of anger is an indicator of emotional struggles within, but I didn't know that. The clamour inside my head was loud and constant. It was exhausting. This was my earliest awareness of one of my companions in life – my inner critic – and believe me, this is one companion that you don't want to have. You may be aware of this harsh and critical voice through your own experience.

This constant battle with guilt ultimately led me to make a personal commitment to follow Jesus when I was sixteen. This occurred at an interdenominational youth camp, where I experienced some significant revelations. I learnt that in order to live a changed life, I needed to invite Jesus into my life and, more importantly, into my heart. I had believed I was a Christian because I went to Sunday school, and then to church. I didn't realise that a relationship with God was a result of the invitation that He extends to us through the life and death of His son. The most compelling realisation I had, however, was that through my own strength and ability I could never be good enough – for myself, for others or for God. I needed to accept that I would continue to fail and stuff up, because that is part of the human condition. We all fail; I was not alone in this. Understanding that Jesus had already won the battle for me, that it was through his love for me and the sacrifice of his life that I was good enough for God, resulted in a major shift in my thinking.

After this experience, I felt more at peace within myself and with others. I was on a personal high for a long time. But then life, as it does, got in the way. There were many more life lessons to learn.

After spending my high-school years as a conscientious student, my life took a turn for the worse when, at the age of seventeen, I met a twenty-one-year-old guy on a blind date. My first opinions of him weren't positive; I didn't even really like him. But he was tall, dark and handsome, and he pursued me. It flattered me and, besides, it was what I had always wanted: a cool, good-looking guy who wanted to be my boyfriend.

What happened over the next nine months was a nightmare. The relationship was traumatic and violent. I was young and naive – an innocent – and I was totally out of my depth. My circle of friends didn't approve of this boyfriend because he wasn't a Christian. And, due to his character and not having a job or a car, my parents didn't approve of him either. I actually agreed with them, but it took me a while to be ready to end the relationship.

One day, I asked him to come along to my church. I was really happy that he agreed, and I felt hopeful that maybe our relationship could work. When we arrived home, my parents were out and we had a disagreement. We were in my bedroom, and he slapped me across the face and pushed me, and I fell onto the edge of a table. He was instantly penitent. I was in shock. This was my first experience of physical violence and I felt frightened and alone. I ended up with a black eye, but I didn't feel as though I could tell anyone about what had really happened, so I made up some story. I remember my parents coming home and Mum looking at me closely, trying to work out what had really happened. I was too ashamed to tell her what happened – that day and at other times. I felt trapped. I did a lot of helpless crying during this time in my life.

Another evening, we went to a local club, then he refused to allow me to go home. He took me to a hotel room and when I said that I had to leave because my parents would be worried, he became angry and barred the exit. He refused to let me ring my parents. The next few hours were awful. I was anxious and afraid, and I knew that Mum would be really worried. Finally, I convinced him to let me go and I caught a taxi home. When I arrived home in the early hours of the morning, Mum confronted me in anger and shock. I was too scared to tell her what had really happened, so I made up some other story. My mother slapped me across the face. Now I felt twice punished. I'd already been punished by him for not doing what he wanted, now I had been punished by Mum for trying to hide what was really happening. And I felt so ashamed. I was, I now know, experiencing a domestic violence relationship.* He took control over my life and, over the course of our relationship, eroded my relationships with family and friends, isolating me from them, as well as damaging any shreds of self-esteem I possessed.

I am including this as part of my story because it exemplifies what can happen to young girls who have low self-esteem, especially when they feel invisible and unattractive. It is a classic case of predator and prey. In my heart of hearts, I knew that this guy was not a good choice, but I was flattered by his attention and interest, and I allowed my life to be taken over by him. It was a scary, difficult and emotionally challenging time. My life took an abrupt U-turn and dumped me in a foreign land.

I met this guy during my term three school holidays, my final term before sitting the Higher School Certificate (HSC). I had done well

---

* Domestic violence is a term used in relation to violence, abuse and intimidation between people who are currently or have previously been in an intimate relationship. It is primarily an imbalance of power, where one person seeks to control the other. It may include, but is not limited to, physical, verbal, emotional, sexual, social, financial and spiritual abuse, and may be directed in person, or by technology, such as by phone, email or social media. It causes fear, and physical and/or psychological harm. It may lead to post-traumatic stress disorder (PTSD).

in the trial exams, so I had anticipated going well in the HSC exams also. Unfortunately, I was so absorbed in this relationship that I didn't put time and energy into preparing for my exams. I matriculated and was accepted into university, but I did not gain results that reflected all the hard work that I'd put into my school years. It was a crushing disappointment and led to me making different life choices than I had originally planned. Instead of going to university, I joined the public service and became an accounts clerk, the most boring job I have ever done. It was meant to be a stop-gap measure until I worked out what I wanted to do with my life.

The consequences of this relationship and the choices I had made led to an even bigger dose of guilt. Even though I knew that God had forgiven me, I couldn't forgive myself. It has taken years of therapy to have compassion for my seventeen-year-old self and, ultimately, to forgive myself – it's been a long and painful journey.

With my parents' help, I managed to escape this relationship, but only after a couple of frightening months when he stalked me. Afterwards, I was very confused about relationships for a few years and, consequently, had a few difficult and disappointing experiences. However, I was then blessed to meet Tony – safe, loving, loyal, gentle and kind. We were friends first, until our friendship blossomed into love.

Tony and I became inseparable. We had so much fun together, so many good times during our two and a half years of dating. Yet I already knew, within the first few months, that Tony was the best person for me. He just felt right. This brings me to the age of twenty-one, the same age Simone was when she died.

CHAPTER 4

SIMONE AND ME

If you lay the story of Simone's life next to mine, there are clear parallels. Some of these are natural – we share genetic and cultural elements that influence our lives. And, additionally, Simone and I share being the eldest child.

Psychologists have found that there are certain personality variables that are consistent with birth order. While recognising that there are many factors that impact the development of personality, it is widely accepted that firstborn children tend to be reliable, conscientious, structured, cautious, controlling and high achievers. They are diligent and want to be the best at everything they do.[9] They tend to have issues relating to over-responsibility, particularly when they are firstborn daughters. We are raised with an ingrained sense that we should be mature and responsible, and set a good example for our younger siblings. We should step up and take the initiative. Being the firstborn daughter is hard work!

H. Norman Wright explains that firstborn traits are partly due to the impact of enthusiastic first-time parents who want to excel at parenting; unfortunately, their child becomes their guinea pig.[10] He maintains that parents will work hard to ensure that their firstborn reaches all milestones – sitting, standing, walking, talking, potty training – at the proper time or, even better, early. This means that the firstborn child tends to put a high value on achievement.

Simone and I were certainly very conscientious and hardworking, seeking to achieve the best we could. This was evident in our attitude and diligence to our family, school, church and university work, in our enthusiastic approach to doing our best and better – doing over and beyond what was needed, whatever the task. To this day, I value these traits in Simone. I loved her enthusiasm, commitment and passion to do her best, and I understand it.

We both grew up in tight-knit families. In my family of origin, this meant that we spent a lot of time together. Family meals were always held together, around the table, with no television or other distractions. We celebrated all occasions – birthdays, Christmas, Easter and anniversaries – together. We had family holidays together till we were all well into our twenties. Because our nuclear family was alone in Australia, without the structures and supports of the wider family to support us, it meant that there were very strong connections between us.

My experiences of family life were structured, strict and controlling, with high expectations around behaviour and life choices, which is typical of European families. Ever seen the movie, *My Big Fat Greek Wedding*? There are some strong similarities between life in Dutch and Greek families!

The father is the patriarch, the head of the house, and there are some rigid structures about how you live within the family. My dad always called himself the 'king' of his castle. There was little flexibility around how we lived our lives, and there were consequences for frowned-upon behaviours. Some of these are endemic to the generation within which I grew up, while others are cultural. For example, I was not allowed to leave the dinner table to go to the toilet, no matter how urgent the need. It was expected that this should have been seen to before dinner. I was not allowed to talk too much, because my father was tired from work. I was not allowed to leave the table until my plate was clear. This meant many long hours spent at the dinner table because I was stubborn in my refusal not to eat certain foods that I didn't like. From memory, I think I won these silent arguments, because ultimately you can't force a child to eat something they won't eat. I continue not to eat those kinds of foods (such as kidneys, brains, endive or liver) and I never tried to force my children to eat foods that they didn't like.

These experiences in my family not only had a huge influence on the person I became, but also impacted the expectations I brought to my family when I became a parent. David Olson[11] explains how we bring baggage from our family that affects many aspects of the way our own family life evolves. This includes the way we communicate, how we handle (or don't handle) conflict, and intimacy (whether the family has emotional closeness or remains distant and disconnected). So many of what we perceive to be natural beliefs and behaviours have actually evolved from our family of origin.

Thus, I built a close family life that in many ways mirrored the one I had been raised within. However, in response to the strict standards of my family, my husband and I have consciously been somewhat more flexible and relaxed in how we live our lives. Despite this, I think it is fair to say – and my children would concur – that we had reasonably high expectations around the way our children lived their lives and what we saw as acceptable behaviour. We certainly created close family relationships by focusing on structures, such as eating meals together, family prayers and frequent family celebrations.

Another similarity is that both Simone and I were loving and caring big sisters to our younger siblings. We were both the natural leaders of all the childhood games and activities within our families. In our roles, we were both reliable, loving and highly involved in our siblings' lives.

We both experienced overly protective mothers. As you will have gathered from my narrative, I was a protective, involved and absorbed parent to Simone. When I became a mother, I took my new responsibilities very seriously. I wanted to be the best parent I could be. So, in my usual fashion, I put one-hundred-and-fifty per cent into parenting.

I believed that if Simone grew up with any significant physical, intellectual or emotional problems it would be entirely my fault. So, it's no surprise that when Simone was diagnosed with ADHD, it had to be my fault, either through my genes or my parenting failures.

I was constantly on the lookout for issues that may impact Simone's wellbeing. This began with her physical safety: I drove her to school and home every day, not trusting the buses or Simone to do this safely. It continued with her emotional wellbeing: I always wanted to talk to Simone about her experiences at school, her relationships with friends and her after-school activities.

This experience mirrored my own experiences of parenting. Mum was also very protective and worked hard to be the best she could be, within the limits of her health issues and her isolation from her extended family. Yet a protective family dynamic has both positive and negative elements. A protective family creates safety, security, and a stable base for a child to go out into the world and return to their safe place. With the encouragement and support of parents, this increases attachment and trust in the parent and also within the child's developing self. However, being too protective can lead to a child feeling as though the world is an unsafe place, and feelings of inadequacy and dependence on caregivers. This limits the child's ability to be confident, independent and autonomous.[12] This happened to me and is something I fear that I engendered, not only in Simone, but also in my other children, to some extent.

We were both raised in Christian families, so there were the same values, beliefs and high expectations about there being a 'right way' to live your life. A Christian family offers children a wealth of positive ethics and values, with aspirations to be loving, respectful, humble, honest, moral, generous, forgiving, compassionate, just, wise, responsible, kind, content, loyal and committed. It's a wonderful set of values to live by but, in my experience, there's also a lot of pressure to live up to that kind of perfection. In real life, these values can feel impossible to achieve. Trying to live up to them can create problems with perfectionism, leading to a judgemental and critical attitude, towards not only one's own failings, but also, sadly, those of others. It can also lead to becoming a people pleaser – prioritising the other to the detriment of yourself. Long term, this is not a healthy way to live; it's not conducive to optimum mental health.

Having strong Christian beliefs and commitments was a huge component of how both Simone and I saw ourselves. When I think of myself and Simone at the age of sixteen, I see strong similarities in our approach to our faith and the way we lived our lives. We both had an intense black-and-white thinking style. This is a tendency to think in extremes, where someone or something is either all good or all bad, and there is no middle ground, no shades of grey. Developing an acceptance of grey has been part of an ongoing struggle through my life journey and I don't know how Simone would have charted her own. However, understanding this propensity has helped me to have more empathy and understanding for Simone, especially in the areas where we were similar.

We shared similar personality styles. I talked a lot, especially at home where I felt safe and comfortable. I was always getting into trouble for talking too much and too loudly at the dinner table. Simone talked a lot! Often at the dinner table. Especially at home, where she felt safe and comfortable. We were both physically uncoordinated, hated team sports and balls in particular. We were both the last to be chosen for the sports team. We both hated PE, sports days, school swimming and athletics carnivals.

While I have been writing this book, I have often caught myself acting in very similar ways to Simone. These are qualities and behaviours that I have either laughed over or been frustrated by, such as scribbling illegible notes on small pieces of paper. This was something Simone did all the time. Now, I realise that I do the same. As I was writing, I would suddenly be struck by an idea or inspiration, and I would quickly jot it down. At times, my desk and office have been littered by small notes, part of myriad ideas, thoughts or quotes that I wanted to use in writing this book. Also, I struggle to limit how much I say, because I want to express it all! To condense is hard work for me, just as it was for Simone.

In my passion for counselling and personal development, I see the same passion that Simone had for God and for art. In her enthusiasm and commitment to the church and serving others, I see my commitment to helping others, including writing this book. It is a joy for me to notice the positive aspects of the similarities that we shared.

Simone and I were both perceived as 'different'. I think this is a crucial parallel in our stories. We were both quiet, shy and introverted outside the home, particularly at school. We both struggled to make friends, without knowing or understanding why. We were both rejected from the upper stratum of the school hierarchy. We both experienced bullying. We both shared a sense of awkwardness within ourselves. I can see it when I look at and compare our childhood photos. There is the same awkward stance and appearance, while our eager and enthusiastic eyes shine earnestly. This similarity is significant in the way that I viewed Simone. Because I had issues with my own experiences of being different, it caused me to struggle and feel negative about her experiences of being different. I looked at her through the eyes of the world, rather than through the positive, empathic experience of my own eyes. I saw in her the shadow side of myself, which I both hated and disowned.

At this point in my life (when Simone was at school), I was nowhere near a state of self-acceptance or self-compassion. I disliked so many aspects of myself. I was still at war within myself, and had split myself into separate parts, simply to survive. I feel sad now to realise that if I had been able to have self-love and acceptance, I could have passed this on not just to Simone, but to all my children. This self-assurance would have placed them in a much healthier and happier place. But, alas, you cannot pass on what you have not yet learned.

We both lived with ADHD. I believe that this is a fundamental similarity between us; diagnosed in Simone's case in childhood, at the age of eight, diagnosed in mine when I was in my thirties. When Simone was diagnosed with ADHD, I had one of those light-bulb moments. All of a sudden, the confusing and disappointing aspects of my life that I had struggled with started to fit together and make sense. Not only did Simone have ADHD, but *so did I*. I remembered my awkwardness, my struggles with attention, my lack of understanding of social cues, my lack of coordination and my early learning difficulties, just to name a few. ADHD is a genetically acquired syndrome, and I was the common denominator, so to speak. I took myself off to be assessed, and was given the diagnosis of ADHD, predominantly inattentive.

Fundamentally, I believe it is due to both the primary and secondary impacts of ADHD that our life experiences resonate with each other. It is the secondary impacts – the emotional and psychological – that have had a huge impact on my life with and without Simone. The consequences of these struggles cause children to feel inadequate, different, weird and not good enough. These feelings are the breeding grounds for anxiety and depression. I will discuss this further when I focus on describing ADHD and how it impacts girls' lives.*

We both lived with a parent who had chronic ill health. I experienced significant trauma living in the shadow of my mother's chronic physical ill health, her life-threatening surgeries, and living away from home as an eight-year-old, with strangers. These were all experiences of abandonment.[13] And abandonment has a major impact on how children develop, influencing their sense of self-worth and security. While Simone did not have a parent with chronic physical ill health, she did have a parent with chronic mental ill health. This means that we both had parents who were not always emotionally available, as a consequence of being unwell. Both Mum and I had little mental headspace to deal as effectively as we would have liked with our children's needs. This was not deliberate, but it still led to experiences of emotional abandonment.

---

* See About ADHD on page 194 for more information.

While there were all these similarities that influenced the way that I parented Simone, I think the *differences* in our lives were also significant in how they influenced our individual emotional experiences.

Growing up as the child of immigrants, without family support, meant that I had less individual support. There was only my sick mother, my absent father and two younger brothers. Visits from extended family were limited, only occurring when I was in my late teens and just by two of Mum's sisters, none of Dad's family. Whereas Simone grew up with a very loving and supportive wider family (grandparents, aunts and uncles), who were involved in our lives and able to give her individual love and attention. They attended birthdays, school award days and sporting events, as well as most of the significant milestones and achievements in her life.

Simone didn't contend with any of the cultural confusion that I experienced. I've always felt as though I was a blend of Dutch and Australian, which is not altogether a bad thing. There is a richness and depth that comes with having diverse cultural experiences. However, there are also struggles related to subtle cultural differences – in outlook and lifestyle – and the differences in language meant that I often felt as if I was caught between two worlds.

In terms of character, Simone was a lot tougher than I was. I could be hurt easily and really cared about what people thought of me. For a long time in my life, I likened myself to a chameleon – a creature that can change its appearance in order to fit in with its environment. I was a people pleaser, who adapted to what people wanted, in order to gain love and affection.

Simone always followed her own path. As described earlier, Simone did not allow others' opinions, prejudices or judgements to affect her actions and behaviour. She remained true to herself and would often push herself outside her comfort zone if she wanted to do something. If her friends didn't want to do it with her, she would still do it. I struggled with this, as I needed the company of friends in order to try new things. Simone was also a lot more adventurous than me. I always need the comfort and security of the known. Simone would bravely drive wherever she wanted to go. I still struggle with driving outside of my own area.

As discussed in my narrative about family experiences, my mother struggled with showing affection. She also struggled with words. I remember often asking Mum about how she felt about something I had done or achieved, because what I wanted was her excitement or enthusiasm, to show me that she cared. But Mum struggled to do this. Time and time again, my mum would say to me, 'I can't do that Connie. You know that, but I am [happy or proud or whatever else it was].' This was disappointing for me, and was something I was able to do with Simone. As words of affirmation are so important to me, and also come quite naturally, I would tell Simone how proud I was of what she had done, and I made a concerted effort to show excitement and enthusiasm about her interests and achievements.

Gifts were another problem. My parents struggled financially on one income. They couldn't afford to buy us many gifts. As an adult, I can understand that, but as a child I felt that receiving one present only was a sign that my parents didn't care about me. Especially when I compared my Christmas or birthday booty with that of my friends. I probably went to the other extreme with my children. I started lay-bying Christmas presents in August (when we were living largely on one salary), so that I could buy a multitude of gifts for the kids.

The experience of feeling loved is directly connected to how love is expressed and then internalised, and this applies to both children and adults. Gary Chapman has written about the concept of love languages for both types of relationships.¹⁴ He describes five languages that people use to express love. These are: words of affirmation, physical touch, quality time, gifts and acts of service. Each individual has different ways of feeling loved and expressing love. All five love languages are important, but individuals tend to have preferred love languages, those that speak to them more loudly than others. Usually, the way that a person expresses their love language is also the way in which they feel most loved. For example, my primary love language is words of affirmation, followed by physical touch and gifts. When someone speaks words of affirmation, acknowledgement or praise, I fly high on love. If they offer gifts, it is important to me because they have taken the time and care to choose something that they think I will like. And who doesn't like hugs? It is no surprise then that the way I express love is through words of affirmation, gifts and physical touch.

As I missed out on all these gifts of love from my parents, I was determined to be a different parent; I would give my children lots of affection and words of praise, and I'd shower them with gifts. So, I showed love to Simone (and my other three children) in these three ways. Did Simone feel loved by these things? I suspect that her strongest language of love was quality time.

I remember that Simone would be visibly brighter, happier and more enthusiastic when I'd spent time with her. When she was younger, it would be taking her to a park, playing with her, reading to her or just spending time together. As she grew older, it would be shopping days, time out for tea and conversation, going for bushwalks or to art galleries. I have to confess that quality time was the weakest of my love languages. I was a time zealot. Being busy with four children, a job, a home and studies meant that my time was limited. I never had enough of it, and so this expression of my love was not as plentiful as the others.

Additionally, I'd had two significant experiences of trauma. The trauma of my mother's illness and the separation from her. And the trauma of a violent relationship when I was still very young. Trauma leaves footprints on the mind, body, spirit and soul. It damages and erodes from the inside out. What we know about trauma is that it may often lead to anxiety, depression and post-traumatic stress disorder (PTSD).

Although I worried that Simone would make similar bad choices to me when she was sixteen, she didn't. Huge sigh of relief. Due to this, Simone did not experience the kind of internal emotional bruises that scar the soul and spirit, as I did. Thankfully, this meant that her experience of the world was somewhat different than it was for me.

Similarities and differences shaped each of our lives and the complexities of our relationship. I have found it extraordinarily helpful to consider them both. They have helped me to put all the pieces of our complicated mother–daughter puzzle into some kind of order, a meaningful shape. This has enabled me, above all, to have empathy and compassion for Simone, my mother and myself. And that's a gift you can't put a price on.

Mum and Dad on their wedding day, 7 December 1958. The Dutch custom is for the groom to pick up the bride and bring her to the church.

Connie, aged 3.

Year 1 school photo, aged 6. I'm in the front row, far right. It seems to me that I look 'odd'.

Family photo at the Camellia Gardens, Caringbah, early 1970s.

Below: Professional photo for Dutch relatives: Connie (12), John (8), Danny (4).

En route to Holland for our 3-month holiday. This photo was taken by KLM for the airline's magazine. The caption says: 'Eight-year-old Connie Hamerslag from Caringbah, NSW, on her way to Schiedam ... Fortunately, her favourite doll was allowed to come, too.'

My 21st birthday celebration at a restaurant in Cronulla (with Tony in the background).

At home with Mum and Dad on my wedding day, 14 May 1983. Note the Dutch pictures in the background.

The happy couple: Connie (21), Tony (22). Taken at the Waterfront Lounge, Sylvania, where we held our reception.

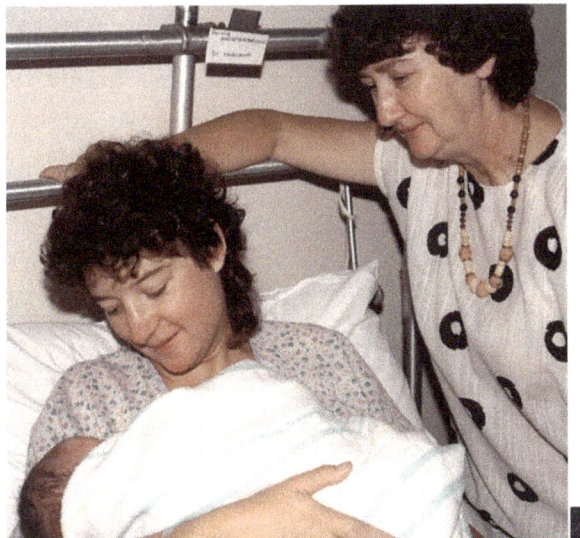

Three generations of mothers and daughters – Mum, me and Simone – on the day of Simone's birth, 17 March 1987.

Simone (2) as the flower girl for Danny's wedding.

Me (8 months pregnant with Daniel) and Simone (3). She was very excited about becoming a big sister.

Simone (3) and Daniel (6 months). She loved this outfit with its matching hat. So did I!

Family photo in our front yard: Simone (9), Daniel (6), Laura (4 months).

Dress ups with family and friends (left to right): Laura, Daniel, Michelle, Emma, Kelly and Simone. Simone is holding a harp she'd made at school.

Simone's HSC graduation day, 2004. Simone is holding her certificates of merit and medal for coming first in visual arts.

Above: Mother and daughter, March 2002.

Left: Simone on our deck on her 19th birthday. I love the way this photo shows her beautiful long hair.

Above: Connie's Bachelor of Social Sciences graduation day, Southern Cross University, 2005.

Top: Simone's Bachelor of Creative Arts graduation day, University of Wollongong, 2007.

Above: Simone on her 21st birthday.

Left: Simone in her favourite arty jeans. This photo featured in the University of Wollongong yearbook, 2007.

One of Simone's major artworks for her Deadman's Creek exhibition.

Simone painting on site for her major work (Bachelor of Creative Arts), Deadman's Creek, Heathcote Road, Sandy Point.

CHAPTER 5

MARRIAGE AND CHILDREN

I was a very young twenty-one when I married, what you might call a late bloomer. I was still an innocent in so many ways. In retrospect, I was quite immature and dependent on my husband. It was as though I simply transferred my reliance straight from my overprotective mother onto my new husband.

Our first years of marriage were very special, and I treasure many happy memories from this time together, when we were free of many of the responsibilities that come with having children. We both worked full-time and studied part-time. We lived in a unit, not far from either of our families, so we enjoyed their support. We also had some wonderful travelling experiences. After eighteen months of marriage, we visited my family in Holland (a cherished dream of mine) and travelled around Europe and Great Britain for nearly three months. It was wonderful to connect with my greater family in Holland and to share an amazing adventure together.

We also did some travelling around Australia, camping around Queensland, Victoria and South Australia. Our travels strengthened our relationship and increased my feelings of safety and security with my husband.

I was twenty-five when I fell pregnant with Simone. This wasn't quite part of our plan at the time. I had an unfulfilled dream of pursuing social work, and had recently started studying part-time at the University of New South Wales, with the intention of gaining a Bachelor of Arts, majoring in psychology and sociology.

I wasn't one of those girls who couldn't wait to have babies. Yes, I definitely wanted children; I would have been heartbroken if I couldn't have any. I just wasn't one of those real clucky types of women, or maybe I just hadn't reached that point in my life yet. My aspirations at the time were to complete my university studies and work in a field where I could make a difference. I wanted to make my mark on the world, to help people and make the world a better place. To be honest, I don't think I was ready – emotionally, intellectually or in terms of maturity – to start a family. Having said that, is anyone really ready to become a parent? It has to be one of the toughest jobs there is. If I knew what was in store and how my life would change, would I have postponed starting a family indefinitely, as some women do these days? I don't know.

Anyway, once we recovered from the shock of finding out we were pregnant, we were both excited and enthusiastic about becoming parents. So, after completing my current semester at university, I put my studies on hold, to return to later.

When Simone was born, I was in awe of the miracle of birth and was enraptured with my new baby daughter. I couldn't stop looking at her. It was as if I needed visible proof that she was really there. While in hospital, I had to have her facing me at all times. If a nurse turned her crib away, I would turn it back again so that I could see her face. I was still trying to absorb that this beautiful baby girl was mine and was here to stay. I was really happy to have a girl. Being the only daughter in my family, I had always wanted a sister. The name Simone was suggested by a work colleague. It wasn't a name I was familiar with – to me, it was a unique name, a name that you didn't hear every day. Tony and I agreed, deciding on this name for our beautiful baby girl.

The first signs of the parenting journey to come started on day five of Simone's life. I experienced what is commonly known as the baby blues.* On the night before I was due to leave the hospital, I was suddenly overwhelmed with fear. I began crying and felt a huge sense of anxiety. The responsibility of taking this precious little baby home became all-consuming. In between bouts of crying, I lashed out at my husband. 'How are you going to help me with this baby when all you do is fiddle with everything?' I had never noticed until now that my husband had a habit of fiddling with whatever was close at hand. It irritated me inordinately. Poor Tony! All of a sudden, he had to deal with an irrational, overwrought woman. I was so destabilised that the hospital decided to keep me in for another twenty-four hours and, when I was sent home, a community nurse was assigned to visit me regularly to provide support.

Although this reaction to childbirth is so common that it is considered normal, it also reflects the enormous responsibility I felt bringing

---

* The baby blues generally happen somewhere between the third and fifth day after birth and are due to hormonal changes. They may include weepiness, feelings of distress and/or fears of an inability to cope with your baby. They usually pass in a short period of time. If they continue, or become more severe, medical intervention is required, as they may have become a more serious form of postpartum depression.

Simone home. And how much I relied on Tony for support. My early experiences of parenting were a messy combination of love and fear. I had fallen head over heels in love with Simone, but I struggled to have confidence in my ability to look after her. A conflicting web of feelings whirled inside me – love, joy and delight mixed up with fatigue, frustration, worry, guilt, confusion and doubt.

Every person I spoke to had different advice, especially the two most important ones – my mother and my mother-in-law. I had no prior experience of babies or children, so I didn't feel as though I had any idea of what I was doing. I struggled with the whole experience of motherhood. I was consistently worried about 'doing things right'. I worried about whether Simone was reaching her developmental goals – crawling, walking, communicating. I worried about her health, taking her to the doctor whenever she had a cold or ailment. I worried about nearly everything, come to think of it.

I was a committed and conscientious mother. I followed my Bible, and Penelope Leach's book *Baby and Child*[15] was a great resource that I dived into regularly. Whenever Simone reached a new stage of development, I checked what Penelope had to say. But sometimes my conscientiousness was a curse, leading to helicopter parenting.* I also read every parenting book I could get my hands on, consistently comparing myself negatively to what I read or what I observed in other mothers.

Some of these feelings I can put down to being a first-time mum, cutting my 'mothering teeth' on my firstborn child. As previously discussed, the first child is often the focus of zealous perfectionist parenting, with some of those standards dropping as you go along.

---

* Helicopter parenting is a term for an overly protective parent, one who goes beyond the ideal level of protectiveness.

I was idealistic, striving towards being some kind of Utopian, perfect mother, and then struggled to live up to my own high standards. I now realise that no one would be able to live up to them.

It was all such hard work. Just getting dressed and out of the door felt like a marathon effort. I struggled with feeling unproductive – because it was so hard to get much done – and as achievement usually boosts my self-esteem, this was an additional challenge.

I also felt lonely and isolated. I was the first among my group of friends to have a child, so I didn't have anyone I could speak to honestly and comfortably about how I was feeling. And I found every day a chore, something to be endured. I would wait impatiently for Tony to come home, to relieve me of the burden of caring for Simone full-time. I missed my friends and work colleagues; I missed the challenge of my working life.

I felt bored and unstimulated, and I had nothing to look forward to. In the lead up to Christmas, when I realised that the main excitement in my life was going to the letterbox in the hope of receiving Christmas cards, I knew that my life had sunk pretty low. If this was the only excitement in my day, there was something wrong. Then I felt guilty and ashamed for feeling this way. That there must be something wrong with me to feel so sad, bored and unhappy.

As much as I loved my daughter and was proud of her, during that first year I became increasingly depressed, and was eventually diagnosed with postnatal depression. I accessed counselling at the time, but I can't remember it making much of a difference. I am a big proponent of counselling, but it's important to find a counsellor with whom you have a good fit, and that wasn't the case on this occasion.

Fortunately, I started to make friends with other young mums through the church and this was a godsend. It kept me sane and helped me to realise that I wasn't alone. All mums, new and experienced, struggle. But it was going back to work part-time that helped most. It gave me a break from full-time parenting and restored some balance in my life. It felt good to be working, and achieving success seemed more straightforward in the workforce than it was as a full-time mother. Gradually, the symptoms of depression and anxiety receded.

After eighteen months, Tony and I decided to have a second child. Although I struggled with parenting, I love babies, so I was happy to find myself pregnant again.

During labour, I remember feeling so excited about Simone meeting her new sibling. Finding out that I'd given birth to a boy was no big surprise, because I'd felt strongly during the pregnancy that I would have a son, and his name would be Daniel. Introducing Daniel to Simone was a beautiful and emotional experience. I was very happy. Our family was complete! (Or so I thought …)

Simone was a loving and attentive big sister. From memory, I had no problems with sibling rivalry, jealousy or tantrums. What was difficult was Daniel. He had health and wellbeing issues, suffering from colic, reflux and sleeping difficulties, and he was often sick. Being the second child, he often caught the colds and viruses that Simone would bring home from preschool. For the first six months, we almost wore holes in the carpet, as we walked around the room trying to settle his colic in any way we could.

Getting Daniel to sleep felt like a mammoth operation. After feeding, I would try to settle him to sleep by patting his bottom, a technique I had learnt from my mother-in-law. This ended up being a burden, rather than a godsend, though, because then the only way he would sleep was if he was patted regularly or his back was rubbed.

Another problem was how to keep Simone entertained *and* out of the bedroom. At this time, they shared a bedroom, so I needed to be prepared and organised. I would set Simone up with some activity, usually an arty/crafty one, and tell her firmly and insistently that no matter what, she was *not* to come into the bedroom, because it would wake her brother up. Which it did. Every time.

Yet, no matter how hard I tried to impress upon Simone that it was important not to disturb me when I was putting Daniel to bed, she would forget, or would need something, or would have to tell me something, and then Daniel would wake. This was very frustrating!

When Daniel was about ten months old, I was again diagnosed with postnatal depression. I was offered medication by my GP, but, in those days, only the short-acting kind, which can become addictive, was available. I didn't want to become dependent on this kind of medication, so it was a short-lived treatment plan.

The first three years with Daniel were tough: he was not an easy child. He was sensitive to the world, both within himself and externally. He had tantrums, particularly during the terrible twos. Many times, I would leave a store in a rush because he was making a scene. He wanted that soft, furry, blue dinosaur, and he was not going to leave the shop without it. Or, he would not drink out of any cup other than his blue sparkly DANIEL one! If you're a mum, I am sure you can relate to these, or similar, experiences.

These were not problems that I'd experienced with Simone. Daniel was also slow to speak and needed speech therapy for a few years, which made communication with him difficult. He was very sensitive to the feel of fabrics – if he didn't like the feel of the material on his skin, he wouldn't wear it. He was resistant to change and it would take him many weeks to adjust to the change from summer to winter clothing.

It would be a hot day and he would insist on wearing track pants and jumpers. Yes, he was a HSP, just like me. I didn't know what it was called back then, but he certainly fits the criteria. So, yes, he was hard work. And how did I cope with his needs? A lot better than I coped with Simone (aged three at the time), as much as I hate to admit it.

While Daniel was more difficult to parent, I was able to ensure that my frustrations didn't impact him. He was just a baby, after all. Unfortunately, the vexation I felt was directed at Simone. If I was having trouble feeding or caring for Daniel while trying to get Simone ready for preschool and, later, school – an exercise requiring vast amounts of patience – if I lost my temper somewhere along the line, Simone was the one who bore the brunt of my frustration. I certainly never physically abused Simone but, because I was stressed, I would get angry, shout and carry on. Later, I would feel guilty and troubled for the rest of the day. I would be anxious to see Simone and apologise to her but, nine times out of ten, Simone seemed to have forgotten. She would smile at me in her absent-minded way and say, 'Don't worry, Mum, I forgot.'

One of my responses to my behaviour was to compare myself to other mothers. Of course, I only compared myself to those mothers whom I thought demonstrated admirable parenting standards. Often, I would compare myself to my best friend Libby, and I never felt like I was doing a good enough job. Comparing yourself to others is a sure way of making yourself feel worse, especially when you only see their public persona. I remember thinking to myself, *Why can't I be more like her? I thought I was a nice person, until I had kids. What happened to me? Who is this angry, unhappy woman?*

By the time Daniel was three, I was not in a good place. I was struggling mightily with a vicious cycle of stress, anger, guilt and shame.

I became clinically depressed and, on my doctor's advice, started anti-depressant medication and began seeing a psychologist. This time, it was a good fit, and my therapist helped me to process the huge burden of guilt I was feeling. One of the most helpful things I learnt was that I was not alone, that other mothers, too, struggled with anger, guilt and shame.

During these sessions, I began to learn that many of my parenting struggles stemmed from my experience of being a child and the relationships I had with my parents. Initially, I didn't understand it all, but as my self-awareness grew, it started to make more sense. Yet, it took some time to integrate what I was learning well enough for it to make a difference to my parenting skills.

Although Daniel was a lot harder to parent than Simone, I seemed to adjust better. I'm not entirely sure why I responded differently, but it was probably a combination of reasons. The gender issue changed things – I have read that this can be the case for parents. I felt a real softness, a tenderness, towards Daniel. I also felt more confident as a parent the second time around. I had learnt what not to do, and I fervently wanted to do a better job. Crucially, I felt an affinity with Daniel. I had an inbuilt sense about what made him tick. Simone was an enigma. I had no sense of innate understanding; often, I simply couldn't figure her out.

Upon reflection, and based on what I wrote in my journals at that time, the triggers for me were feeling overwhelmed and time pressure, which both caused me stress. I had a low stress tolerance, and still do. Whenever I had too much to do, especially when there were time constraints, such as trying to get the kids to school before that 9.30 am bell, or get them ready before the school bus arrived, my tolerance level lowered very quickly. The more demands on my time, and the more that I needed to get done (actual or perceived tasks, because I am a perfectionist), the more stressed I became.

I found it really hard to leave the house for the day if the dishes weren't washed, the beds made and the kids' toys tidied away. Doing these tasks made me feel more in control, which helped me feel good superficially. Yet, on a deeper level, I was less in control, because my emotions were controlling me. As my stress levels increase, so does my frustration. And the more frustrated I became, the more I would shout. The more I would shout, the more my anger was triggered, especially because, by then, I would feel guilty about becoming angry. I would try so hard to be patient but, more times than not, I would lose it. What happens when I lose it? I shout, I swear, I argue, I demand, I bribe. I become a person that I really don't like.

I particularly hated it when I would swear. Swearing did not fit with my value system. I condemned and punished myself for swearing, but I kept on doing it. Swearing seemed to release the anger and frustration that I was feeling. (Just to be clear, I didn't swear at my kids, I swore at myself, at the frustration that I was feeling.) In order to work on this problem, I read self-help books about anger. I tried various strategies and I sought insight from my counsellor. I would try to count to ten, I would leave the room, I would breathe and I would talk to myself (in a critical, rather than a compassionate voice, which, I now know, would have been more helpful).

Sometimes these strategies worked. Well, they would work for the first, second, maybe third frustrating provocation (e.g. kids not listening, kids not getting ready, the baby crying), but by the nth time, I would give up and vent my frustration.

I now know that anger is a sign of inner turmoil and, often, negative self-experience. When I meet an angry, reactive person, I know that there are usually unmet childhood needs lurking beneath the anger. There may also be fear, grief, anxiety, sadness and self-criticism. For me, it was all of them, but primarily fear and anxiety. I was afraid of being a bad mother and having a negative impact on my kids' psyches. I was afraid of the responsibility of bringing up my kids and doing a good job of it. I was afraid of my anger, a towering monster that I could not control. I knew what I was doing was wrong, but I felt powerless to control it. Now, I have compassion for an angry person, but, back then, there was no way I could have compassion for my angry self. All I did was judge it. This was *not-good-enough parenting*! It was unacceptable.

I wonder now why I never considered going to a parenting education class or support group. Maybe there weren't many available at the time. In any case, it didn't occur to me. I just kept on reading parenting or self-help books. And complaining! Why couldn't I follow some basic parenting common sense? Separate your child from their problem. Blame the behaviour, not the child. Why couldn't I do it?

CHAPTER 6

AND THEN THERE WERE MORE

When Simone was eight and Daniel was five, I discovered that I was pregnant again. Although Tony and I had discussed the idea of having another child, we couldn't commit to following through with a clear decision. We were blessed with both a son and a daughter, and to have another child, financially and logistically, would be a stretch. At this time, I was working part-time at a local university library. It was a job that I loved, with a gentle and caring team of librarians. I had returned to my university studies, after an eight-year break, and was studying psychology, externally, through Southern Cross University.

I was also running a mother's support group called SHARE at our local church. This was my brainchild, and was an attempt to support mothers, like me, who wanted advice and the direction of experts to help us become the best parents we could be. It involved inviting speakers to discuss a variety of topics that were relevant to young mums. Life was full and busy.

I was still struggling with managing my emotions, but I was feeling more empowered than in earlier years. Having a supportive and caring husband was a major contributor in helping me to manage all aspects of my life. Tony has always been a hands-on dad, or a Renaissance man, as my friends called him. He has always helped with looking after the kids, the housework and the cooking when I was working or studying. Without his practical and emotional support, I wouldn't have been able to handle the many balls that I was juggling at the time.

On the day I found out I was pregnant, while surprised I was also overjoyed. Tony and I both were. I secretly hoped for another daughter. It was a lot more tiring being pregnant the third time around, but I was hopeful and excited about a new addition to our family.

The day of the birth was both dramatic and ecstatic. Dramatic, because Laura became distressed during labour, which required intervention with forceps and a humidicrib after birth, as she was struggling with breathing. My first impression of Laura was of how frightened she looked; I recalled this in later years, when Laura experienced significant anxiety. The day was ecstatic because I had a lovely baby daughter! I felt that God had given me a second chance, an opportunity to redeem myself. I needed to prove to myself that I could bring up a daughter in a way that was more congruent with my values – to be patient, loving and kind, to have more control over my anger, to avoid swearing and cursing when I became frustrated. And, most importantly, to love and accept Laura, exactly as she was. Although my understanding of this element of parenting wasn't fully developed, I had a nascent awareness of its value.

Changing my mindset really helped me to value and appreciate Laura. I constantly reminded myself how lucky I was to have another daughter. I focused on all the positive aspects of Laura's being and ignored the negative. Fortunately for me, Laura was a very happy and delightful baby. She was the earliest to smile, smiling at me at just three weeks old.

She was not, however, a good sleeper – forty minutes was her limit. This made life busy and stretched. Having three children, of course, makes life busier anyway and there wasn't much time to rest or be as organised as I would have liked. But I was determined to accept Laura completely. If she didn't want to sleep, so be it. I was not going to force the issue.

Laura was a quick learner, too, the earliest of my children to reach the milestones of crawling (six months) and walking (eleven months). Even though she wore a brace for clicky hips,* she still managed to waddle around. I was a very proud parent!

While my experience of parenting Laura was dominated by my intention to parent her differently from Simone, Laura was never an easy child. She was gorgeous, intelligent, full of life and character, cheeky and engaging, but very demanding, both physically and emotionally. She was a 'look at me, Mum' kind of child, all the time. There were many times when I felt frustrated and stretched, but I was determined to be patient and accepting. She was also clumsy, impulsive, excitable, talkative and unpredictable; actually, a lot of the same traits that I had experienced with Simone, but this time around I chose to turn a blind eye to them. I worked so hard not to judge these traits that I didn't recognise them as significant signs of ADHD until much later in Laura's life.

When Laura was about eighteen months old, postnatal depression made a return visit. I blamed my hormones to some extent, as I was struggling with acne and PMS, but I was also overwhelmed with managing three children, work and study. This was the worst

---

* Clicky hips is the common term for congenital dislocation of the hip. It needs to be treated early, as it could otherwise lead to a permanent limp in later life. It is more common among girls than boys.

depression I had experienced. It felt as though I was being held captive in a very dark pit – a huge, black hole in the earth – with slippery slopes that had no hand or foothold, no way to climb out. I cried a lot. I have memories of lying on the lounge and doing nothing at all. This was unusual for me because I was normally task-oriented and felt better when I got things done. But I was too tired; I was exhausted. Tiredness or feelings of exhaustion have now become early warning signs that depression is hovering close by.

It took further counselling, antidepressant medication and lots of self-care to emerge from this depression. As always, Tony was my lifeline. Without his support, I probably would have needed hospitalisation. Friends were a consistent source of encouragement and support, too. Progress was slow; it felt as though I were on an emotional rollercoaster. I had good patches – when I was travelling up the incline – but there were bad times when I came crashing down again.

When Laura was four, Daniel nine and Simone twelve, I became pregnant again. (Yes, I do know about birth control!) This time, the news was harder to take. I wasn't sure how I would manage parenting four children, as I was struggling with three. I had never envisaged or planned on having four children, and I didn't know how I would cope. I was nervous and troubled. However, a new baby is a gift from God and, once I'd wrapped my head around it, I was delighted to welcome Matthew into our family. Now our family was surely complete!

And I did cope, as you do when you have no choice. I certainly learnt how to multitask, though that first year was full-on. But I survived. It surprised me, and it increased my confidence in my ability to manage. It was also fortunate that Matthew was an easy child. He was a good sleeper, had no significant health issues and was easy to parent. He is, to this day, an easygoing guy, so this was in my favour. Yet I sometimes wonder if it's because he's had to be. As the fourth child, he learnt from an early age that he had to fit in and go with the flow.

This time the depression didn't return until Matthew was about two but, in actual fact, I think it was there all along, bubbling beneath the surface and peeking out when life was too much for me. I knew that my depression would have an impact on my children's emotional wellbeing. It worried me a lot, over the years. I had regular counselling, and I was taking antidepressants that helped lessen the severity of the lows, but my inner self was so misshapen by sadness, grief and guilt (always guilt) that I was not able to be the mother I wanted to be.

The guilt that I felt during these tough years of parenting didn't just focus on my lapses of self-control, it attacked every aspect of my being. I struggled so much with being a mother, especially the fact that I didn't naturally enjoy all the (so-called) wonderful elements of mothering. You know, the glorified mother presented on television advertisements for Mother's Day, where a beautiful, serene mother gazes lovingly at her children, rejoicing in putting their needs first.

I hated being stuck at home all the time. I missed the achievements of working, including earning an independent income. I hated missing out on socialising because I was breastfeeding or settling the baby. I wanted to be a selfless, altruistic mother, but I didn't feel those sentiments. I was unable to live up to my own ideal. I gave myself serious talks about the importance of what I was sacrificing for the wellbeing of my children, but it didn't seem to help.

Guilt and shame were my constant companions. My inner critic was working overtime. It pretty well consumed me. The ensuing fallout caused a lifetime battle with what Ita Buttrose and Penny Adams call motherguilt.[16]

Motherguilt was strong in my relationship with Simone, particularly as she became a teenager. A significant issue was listening. Looking back through my journals, Simone not listening was a consistent theme and a constant source of frustration. I took Simone's not listening personally, mistakenly interpreting it as an affront. I didn't consider that maybe she didn't hear me because she was lost in her own internal world, that it wasn't deliberate on her part. Although I did wonder if she was simply tuning me out. If all you hear is complaint and criticism, it is understandable that you don't always want to listen. Instead, I was reactive. Not being listened to is a major trigger for me. Growing up, I rarely felt listened to. In fact, I usually felt invisible or unseen. I was told that I talked too much, or that I needed to focus on helping my mother and considering her needs. It is also how I usually felt at school, both in primary and high school. Invisible, insignificant and unimportant, as I have described.

Another part of my struggle was that I saw a lot of myself in Simone. Some were positive aspects – enthusiasm, commitment, passion – but there were also elements of myself that I didn't like (such as being different – awkward, shy and introverted – general moodiness, and difficulties staying focused and attentive). What confused me was being unable to figure out whether it was the ways in which Simone and I were alike that frustrated me the most, or our differences. It would have been good if I'd read Carl Jung earlier.[17] He discusses the importance of our subconscious mind and how what bothers us in others is often a reflection of what we don't like in ourselves. I needed an awareness of what I didn't like in myself in order to identify what belonged to me and what belonged to Simone. And then I had to make the necessary changes in myself, and have compassion and empathy for Simone's struggles with similar issues.

I asked Tony what he thought was the root of the problem with my relationship with Simone. He thought that I wanted to have some control over her, as her mother, but I could never achieve it because she was as strong-minded as me. Also, that I didn't understand her personality. Tony really did 'get' Simone in ways that I didn't. He seemed to have a similar innate understanding of her as I had with Daniel.

As Simone grew older, we often butted heads. As Tony observed, we were both stubborn and determined, and we both wanted to have the last word in an argument and be right. We were both moody and temperamental. It was like two teenaged siblings fighting for supremacy! Tony and our other kids had learnt to withdraw and not enter into arguments with me, but Simone would fight and would not back down. I wish I had taken more responsibility for my behaviour back then. I should have focused on being the responsible adult, on stepping up and changing my behaviour. Back then, however, I was blinded by my own painful emotional experiences and lacked self-awareness.

One area we fought about consistently was tidiness. I know, it seems trivial and unimportant, but it has always been an issue for me. I like to keep a tidy house. To be honest, I probably lean towards the obsessive–compulsive side of the spectrum. If my house is tidy and in order, it makes me feel more in control; I can breathe more easily.

Simone was not tidy. Being tidy didn't enter into Simone's consciousness; on the contrary, it had no significance. Disorganisation, including messiness, is a key characteristic of ADHD (in this case, one that I didn't share). Simone's room was habitually chaotic, and this didn't improve as she grew older. You had to pick your way around the room, being careful not to step on something. And her mess was not limited to her bedroom. (Remember the trail of clues I mentioned earlier?) The sense I made of it was that it was probably a combination of her creative mind, her absent-minded nature and a manifestation of ADHD. Or that she just wanted to drive me up the wall!

At the time, I also speculated that my high levels of frustration were due to the fact that Simone was not the kind of daughter that I wanted her to be. I loved her, but I recognised that I had a hard time liking her at times. This is a painful admission to make, but I know that I'm not the only parent who has felt like this.

It wasn't until many years later that I understood my crucial problem in the way I parented Simone – I didn't offer her unconditional love and acceptance. To love Simone, exactly as she was, the good bits and the annoying bits. All of her, the lovely and the unlovely, which is what every child needs. What each and every one of us needs! It is an essential human need to be loved for who we are. This now makes total sense, especially because I never felt unconditionally loved and accepted when I was growing up. And I felt as though the problem lay with me – there was something wrong with me, I was not good enough. And that was the reason for being unable to meet my mother's expectations or those of my peers. This led me to not like myself. And, if you cannot love yourself, how can you love a daughter who, in many ways, is just like you?

It took many years of reading, reflection, learning and therapy for me to deeply acknowledge and understand this.

Eventually, I returned to my university studies, and this gave me a focus outside of parenting. It also made me feel as though I was following one of my dreams – to gain a degree and work in a profession where I would make a difference. It felt meaningful, and gave me something to focus on that wasn't the negative loop in my mind.

I originally started studying psychology and sociology, which I found fascinating. However, after the birth of Matthew, I made the difficult decision to change my major to counselling studies, as I struggled with the statistics component of psychology.

Graduation Day, in late 2005, was a huge milestone, and I felt immensely proud of myself for fulfilling and achieving this dream. It took ten years, on and off, toughing it through the challenges of parenting and depression, but I was so happy that I had persevered and achieved a Bachelor of Social Science. The graduation was a wonderful celebration, attended by my family – our four children, my parents and in-laws – and some of my closest friends. I began looking for opportunities in the counselling field. It was not an easy transition, because my work experience during the previous twenty years was in libraries.

Initially, I became a volunteer telephone counsellor at Lifeline. I then became a supervisor, a coordinator, a group facilitator and, finally, a trainer. This experience enabled me to gain a position at Anglicare, which was the beginning of my paid career in counselling. Since then, I have worked for many counselling agencies, and I also run a small private practice in my local area.

CHAPTER 7

LOSING SIMONE

As I think about losing Simone, I realise that this part of my story began long before 10 September 2008. It started when I began to worry about losing Simone.

During those tumultuous years of raising her, when I alternated between anger, guilt, shame and depression, when my inner critic raged, I worried about something happening to Simone. I worried a lot about the impact my anger would have on her, that she would be psychologically scarred or, worse still, would self-harm or even suicide. I would say to myself, 'If anything ever happens to Simone, it will be my fault.'

I knew from reading multiple books about parenting and, later, from my studies in psychology and counselling of the importance of parenting, of how early life experiences influence the person we become. I also knew firsthand – through my own years of therapy and extensive self-reflection – how my experiences in childhood had shaped me. I knew that I wasn't guilty of the major parental failures, such as neglect or abuse, but I also knew that my anger, my verbal ranting, would have affected her psyche.

When Simone gained her P-plates and ventured into the world on her own, I worried. Whenever Simone was driving, I worried. I'm aware that I'm not the only parent who has concerns when their kids start driving; the media report the high levels of adolescent-driver car accidents frequently, so we all know the risks. I also know from speaking to other parents that they worry about their children on the roads. The loss of control makes it difficult for parents because we cannot protect our kids when they are on the road, alone. This experience is particularly relevant with a firstborn child, as it is with most first-time experiences. This first-time experience, however, has a lot more potential danger. Although I breathe a sigh of relief when any of my children arrive home safely, especially when they have travelled long distances. Naturally, losing Simone in a car accident has increased my anxiety about my children's safety when travelling on the road.

Simone had a couple of failed attempts at gaining her driver's licence. She finally achieved it on her third attempt. She also had two minor car accidents after gaining her P-plates, but neither caused significant damage to the car and none to Simone, at least not physically. Now, of course, I think that this should have been a warning to us about her safety as a driver. Tony had some concerns about her driving skills, but he anticipated that if Simone were to be involved in an accident it would be minor in nature, not occurring at a higher speed and, thus, not causing significant injury. I have since wondered, many times, if we should even have encouraged Simone to drive, knowing her attention difficulties. But then I reason, how would that have been for Simone? To not feel trusted to drive a car, to be independent. How would that have made her feel about herself and her abilities? It wouldn't have been fair. And there are plenty of people with ADHD who don't die at the steering wheel. How could we have treated Simone any differently?

There were other times when Simone experienced driving-related problems, such as the time she parked in the part of the car park that was locked early. And she then tried to climb a very high gate to get out! Simone hadn't seen or read the sign warning of the early closure. Or the time she got lost going to an event in Penrith and somehow ended up at Berowra Waters (near Hornsby). Or the time she ran out of petrol. Or the time she locked her keys in the car and couldn't contact us because we were away for the weekend and had no mobile-phone coverage. While these are the kind of events that can happen to any of us, I always had a fear about how Simone would respond and cope.

For the parent of an ADHD adolescent or young adult driver, our natural parental anxiety is increased, due to the inherent difficulty they have maintaining attention and concentration. As has been reported in the media, by insurance agencies, and through research by universities and paediatricians, the risk of accidents is higher in both teens and adults with ADHD.

I knew that Simone's attention could wander from the road. I'd noticed it as a passenger and heard about it from the other kids. I had even seen it directly, on one occasion, when I passed by her on the road. We were both travelling to Wollongong – Simone to university, me to work. I saw how she was playing with her hair, looking dreamy and vague, and clearly didn't have her full attention on the road.

My anxiety reached an all-time high when Simone was doing her first round of pracs (practical teaching experience). This was a challenging time for Simone, but also for me. She would often be up late at night writing the required lesson material, and then she had to get up early and drive to an unfamiliar area. Simone had always experienced sleeping difficulties (she had trouble turning her brain off at night – another ADHD symptom) and it was worse at this time due to the huge study load she was carrying.

During this time, I was intensely afraid that Simone would have a car accident. I would check in with her by text during the day, to ensure that she had arrived safely at her destination. And I'd wait with bated breath for that reassuring ping that alerted me to an 'I'm okay' message. When I was driving home from work, I would worry about whether Simone's car would be parked at home. I remember visualising her car – a blue Nissan Nomad – sitting in its habitual parking spot in front of our house. I would hold that image in my mind to comfort me. If it wasn't there, my heart would drop and I would have a strong, fearful reaction. When Simone was out, I would often check through the window to see if she was home yet. It's not as if I had a premonition that she would have a car accident, it was more as though I had an expectation that, at some point, an accident would happen. No amount of reassurance from Tony or others helped.

I remember one time when we were going to Mudgee for the weekend with some friends, and Simone had left her mobile phone at home. I had forgotten to give her money for lunch and petrol, and I was worried because I couldn't contact her and I knew she was low on petrol. I worried that she might be stranded on the side of the road and not be able to contact anyone. Due to my high levels of anxiety, we didn't leave for our weekend away until Simone arrived home, much to my great relief. I had been beside myself with worry, to the point that I felt physically sick. In order to get through the afternoon, I did the ironing. Whenever I am going through severe anxiety, I catch up on my ironing. It gives me something specific to focus on. There is something about ironing that I find therapeutic; it's a form of mindfulness for me.

In retrospect, my reactions seem extreme, even for me. But they demonstrate how severe my anxiety was at this time. It was also affecting my sleeping. I would wake up at three in the morning and be unable to get back to sleep, a clear indicator of high anxiety. Ultimately, I saw my doctor and she prescribed antidepressants for my anxiety (which I hadn't been taking for many years), along with counselling. Gradually, I started to feel a bit better. I learnt to trust that God would bring her home safely. I began to have times when I would not worry for longer and longer periods of time. I started to breathe and be at ease.

And then it happened.

Among the huge range of thoughts and feelings that I had, one of them was blaming myself for having stopped worrying. If I had continued to worry, maybe I could have kept her alive. Maybe it was my worry that had protected her, because when I worried I was more proactive in keeping Simone prepared and alert for all possibilities. I had let down my guard and my greatest fear had come to pass.

It had been a big year, for both of us. Simone was working towards her Graduate Diploma in Education, and there was a heavy load of both written assessments and practical teaching placements. I was feeling the stress of this, in addition to my responsibilities with the other children and a new job that I was struggling to adjust to. Only two weeks earlier, I had grimaced into the mirror as I was getting ready for work and said, not for the first time, to God and to anyone else who might listen, 'I don't know how much longer I can take this.' These were not token words. I really meant them.

The night before the accident, I was trying to settle down to sleep. Something wasn't right. I lay in the darkness, straining my ears, conscious of the soft breathing of my husband beside me. It was too quiet. Why couldn't I hear Simone in the upstairs study? This may sound strange, so let me explain. Our study is located directly above our bedroom. When anyone is in there, you can hear them clearly, especially when it is quiet. Usually, when Simone was working on her university projects at night, you could hear her. The floorboards would creak with the movement of the study chair, you would hear the staccato tapping of the keyboard and the restless movements of her walking around the room when she became bored. Had she given up on her uni assignment and gone to bed? No, she couldn't have. She had too much work left to finish, and it was due in two days' time. It was a major paper, worth sixty per cent of her final grade.

I grew suspicious. I whispered to my husband, 'I can't hear Simone. Can you?' There was no response. I tried again, louder this time. 'Simone should be working on her paper and I can't hear her. Can you?' There was a murmured, sleepy response: 'No. Don't worry. Go to sleep.' Go to sleep? How could I? I was too worried about her getting her paper done on time. My body grew tense and uptight, my mind was racing, worrying about her paper and the amount of work that she needed to do. I wondered if she was reading, playing a game on the computer or on Facebook. She wouldn't do that. Would she? No. She couldn't be.

I tried my husband again. 'Tony, can you go upstairs and check on what she is doing? I think that she is playing a game, or reading. You know that if I go, I will get angry.' Tony's response was firm. 'No, she isn't. You go if you're worried. I'm tired. I don't want to go up there.' I waited another few minutes for a sound, or for sleep to come. It was no use. I crept up the stairs and saw the light under the closed door.

Slowly, I opened it. She was on the computer all right, not working on her uni assignment. 'Simone, what are you doing?' I hissed, angrily. 'I can't believe that you are playing The Sims – again! At this time of night, when you should be working on your paper.' I was livid with anger and anxiety. I was so cross that I couldn't think straight. Simone looked at me vaguely and distractedly. 'I'm just having a break. I can't think anymore.' Her expression brightened suddenly, she smiled and laughed. 'Look, Mum, I have started a new Sims Easterbrook family. It's so cool. Look at what I have done …'

Again, I thought. I didn't want to hear about games, I wanted her to focus on finishing her assignment. If not that, then I didn't want to hear about it. Angrily, I insisted that she turn the computer off and go to bed if she wasn't working on her paper. She needed sleep before a big day when she had both university and prac. This scenario was not a new one.

The next morning, Simone told me that she had slept badly. She said that she had lain awake for hours – she had been too hyped up from playing her computer game to go to sleep. She hadn't been ready for sleep, and it was my fault because I had forced her to go to bed.

Upon hearing this, mixed in with my irritation and worry was guilt. So, it was my fault again, I had handled the situation badly. I tried not to listen to the familiar voice from my inner critic. I apologised for my anger of the night before, and I explained about my anxiety about her unfinished assignment. She smiled at me warmly and said that it was okay. I could see that she meant it and I continued getting ready for work.

Simone had a few hours to spare before she needed to go to uni for the day. I expected that she would be at the computer, working on her paper, so I checked in on her, on my way out the door. Was she working at the computer, as I expected? No, there she was, sitting on the floor, reading a big thick fantasy novel. She looked up at me dreamily and explained that she was just reading to relax, before having to deal with the stress of her paper. I was totally exasperated. There was nothing else to say. I wished her good luck with her big day, but I was shaking with irritation and anxious frustration. I felt impotent – why was there nothing I could do or say that would make a difference, that would help her?

It was 10 September 2008 – six short months after Simone's twenty-first birthday. It was now 6.20 pm and it had been another busy day. I had just travelled back from Wollongong, from my work as a counsellor at Anglicare, to lead the training program for the Lifeline volunteer telephone counsellors. I was running late and remember feeling rushed and a little stressed.

I sat for a long moment in my car, to take stock of my day and mentally prepare myself for the evening ahead. I looked around, revelling for a moment in the magic of twilight. I love that too-short interval when the world is poised between day and night – I've always felt that it has almost a mysterious, enchanted feeling about it. The sky was a deep lustrous blue, the colour that morphs into darkness. The first stars were appearing. It was unusually warm for an early spring evening, and I remember feeling the quiet peacefulness of that time of day.

Pushing aside the desire to sit and just be, I hurried into the training room. I felt no sense of foreboding, no warning that my life was about to be irrevocably changed. A few times during the training session, I thought of Simone and wondered how her big day had gone, and whether she was home from uni yet. I knew that she'd driven to a high school on the South Coast, which would add another twenty minutes to her drive home.

I messaged Tony during our break to see if Simone was home. This was not unusual for me, as you now know. Break ended before I heard back, and the evening proceeded normally. I didn't check my phone again until I had finished packing up for the night. I noticed, with surprise, that there were a few missed calls from Tony. I was curious, but not worried. Yet I decided to call him straight away, rather than wait till I got home. As soon as Tony answered the phone, I knew that something was wrong. His voice didn't sound right. I asked him what was wrong, what had happened. He stumbled over his words, and told me that something *had* happened, but that he couldn't tell me over the phone. By this stage, my anxiety was rising quickly. I noticed that my heart was beating so fast that I could hear it in my eardrums. I felt hot, sweaty, agitated and focused. What was going on? What had happened?

Tony said that he would ring me back in a few minutes, that he had to check up about something. I put my phone down beside me, watching and waiting for that return call. By this stage, my training colleagues had noticed that there was something wrong. I don't know exactly how I looked, but I know that I was feeling panicked. I was desperate for Tony to ring back. So desperate that I forgot that my phone was on silent, which meant that I wouldn't be able to hear it. Suddenly, I noticed that it was flashing and, with shaking hands and voice, I answered the phone.

'Tell me what's happened. I can't stand this. You have to tell me.'

Even as I type this now, my hands are trembling and my heart is racing. Tony asked me if I was alone or if I had someone with me.

I couldn't understand why he would ask me such a stupid question, why did it matter whether I had someone with me or not? Tony's voice continued to sound strange and hesitant.

'Yes, of course I do,' I answered. 'The other trainers and facilitators are here.'

'Well then, the police have told me that it is okay to tell you. There has been a car accident and Simone has not made it through. She has died.'

Oh my God! I don't know what I said. I think I screamed, sobbed and shouted. I couldn't make sense of the words he was saying. Tony told me that he and Daniel, my eldest son, were at Wollongong Hospital and he asked if someone could drive me there. He was insistent that I was not to drive myself. I don't know what I said next, but I must have agreed and made some arrangements.

I remember my feelings of intense rage. I threw my phone across the room and I must have screamed and cried out because the other women rushed to me and asked what had happened. It was so hard to talk, to explain, but, somehow, I did.

The kind ladies at training, the Lifeline facilitators, drove me to Wollongong. The trip seemed to take forever. I was very quiet, hardly saying a word the whole trip. But it was extremely noisy in my head. My thoughts were whirling and spinning so fast – shock, disbelief, horror, fear. The physical emotions were horrendous and are difficult to describe. It felt as though my whole body had been sucked inside out and there was also an enormous burden on my back, weighing me down. It felt like I was carrying a huge sack of potatoes, and they were pushing my body downwards, into darkness. I was fearful of passing the accident site; I didn't want to witness any part of the scene. I was terrified of what I might see, of how

Simone's precious body might have been impacted by the accident. My thoughts went around senselessly, a crazy merry-go-round gone into hyperdrive. I wanted the trip to end, but I also dreaded it. I was terror-stricken by what I might see, what I would experience at the end of this horrible journey. We finally arrived.

I couldn't seem to walk, so dear Anne and Teresa walked me to the hospital emergency department. I remember looking around and seeing all these strangers staring at me. I wondered if they knew, whether there was something about how I looked that alerted them to tragedy. We were directed to the small room where Tony and Daniel were waiting. I rushed into their arms and we all howled. It was horrific. I can't describe how terrible it was to hear, feel and see our heartbreak. It was like a nightmare. But also not. It felt too real.

A doctor and a social worker were also waiting in the room. As our sobs quietened, they spoke to me. The doctor explained what had happened. Simone's van had rammed straight into the back of a coal truck, which had been travelling slowly up the hill at Mount Ousley Road, Bellambi, near Wollongong. As far as the emergency responders could tell, Simone didn't see the truck, because there were no skid marks on the road, and there would have been if she had tried to brake. We later learnt that a car had overtaken the truck at around the time that Simone was, perhaps, trying to overtake it herself. When the truck changed down a gear, she went straight into it.

The doctor went on to explain that the ambulance had difficulty accessing the accident site during peak hour. They had tried to send a helicopter but there was nowhere to land. Simone's injuries had been life-threatening. A doctor was travelling in the car behind hers and he had worked hard to stop her bleeding. When the ambulance arrived, there was nothing they could do, because they would have needed to be in surgery in order to save her life. Apparently, it was the same kind of injury that Princess Diana suffered in her fatal car accident. The paramedics worked on saving Simone throughout the twenty-minute trip to the hospital, because she was young and they hoped that maybe she could survive. But despite all this, she was pronounced dead when she arrived at the hospital.

After some time, we were taken to the room where they had laid her body. I was so scared of what I might see. I felt like the walking dead. I was relieved to see that apart from some bruising on her neck and cuts on her face, her body was not shattered or broken, but I didn't want to look too closely.

It was a shock to see her lying silent and still. It was clear that the Simone I knew and loved had left her body; it was only her shell that was left behind. There was no warmth, no softness. I remember stroking her thick golden hair, touching her cold white skin. The sterile, arid air of the hospital felt alien, unreal.

The hospital staff kindly gave us as much time as we needed with Simone, to touch her, hug her, speak to her. This whole scene is indelibly printed on my brain. For years afterwards I would have flashbacks – of Simone lying there, of myself, Tony and Daniel trying to come to grips with what we were seeing. This is a hell I wouldn't wish on anyone. Ever.

Writing this is so hard. It's the first time I have written about the night of her accident, though I have told a few close friends. It feels as though I'm experiencing it all over again. Even now, when I know this has happened, I still can't believe it happened to me, to my Simone. Now and then, when I look at newspaper articles that were written at the time, I have a feeling of surreality, an inability to believe that this really happened to our family.

For Tony, and for our children, memories of the night before we found out were very different. I have found it hard, almost impossible at times, to both hear and imagine how it was for them to learn about Simone's accident. They all recall noticing that Simone was late coming home from uni that day. However, being late was not such a big change for Simone, so they accepted it as normal. Dinner was prepared, and Matthew (our youngest son, who was nine at the time) called out from our deck for Simone to come home for dinner. Loudly. It was all a bit of a joke but, thinking about it now, it feels macabre.

Laura (thirteen at the time) recalls that it was a lovely twilight and the scent of jasmine was in the air. Curiously, she said that it was the first time that she remembers feeling lonely. Simone and Laura had a close bond, both of sisterhood and friendship. As mentioned, Simone enjoyed the company of all her siblings and was very close to them.

After dinner, at around 8.00 pm, as the family settled around the television, they were surprised by a loud knock at the door. Two policemen stood outside. They informed Tony that Simone had been involved in a car accident and that he needed to accompany them to Wollongong Hospital. When Tony asked how Simone was, the policemen didn't answer, they simply repeated that there had been an accident and he needed to come to the hospital. They asked if there was anyone else that could come with him. As I was unreachable at work, Tony asked our son Daniel (eighteen at the time) if he would come. He then went next door, to ask our neighbours if they could stay with our younger children.

Tony said that it was a horrific trip to the hospital. The policemen were silent. He didn't know whether Simone was alive or not. However, when the hospital staff directed him to a small room near the casualty entrance, he knew that what he most feared was true.

Tony works at a hospital, so he knows what *that room* is used for: to tell family and loved ones the bad news.

The trip home from the hospital is a blur. I remember feeling really unsafe in the car as the police drove us home, silence the only sound. All I could think of was how would we tell our children what had happened to their sister. And their grandparents. And everyone else.

The sleepless night that followed seemed endless. My husband and I curled up silently beside each other and attempted to sleep. Telling our kids the next morning, and then our family and friends, was a nightmare. Hearing the devastating cries of my children, my mother-in-law and father-in-law, my dad and my closest friends cannot be adequately described. It was an intense anguish of the spirit. I will never forget that awful day.

Feeling your own pain is hard enough, but bearing the pain of your children, your family and other loved ones is like undergoing the experience all over again. To this day, I hate telling people that my daughter died. Having to deal with their reaction, as well as your own, creates a double whammy, an addition to the painful reminder that this awful thing has happened. It is all too real, too horrible.

CHAPTER 8

GRIEVING SIMONE

Every time we make the decision to love someone, we open ourselves to great suffering, because those we most love cause us not only great joy but also great pain. The greatest pain comes from leaving ... the pain of the leaving can tear us apart.

Still, if we want to avoid the suffering of leaving, we will never experience the joy of loving. And love is stronger than fear, life stronger than death, hope stronger than despair. We have to trust that the risk of loving is always worth taking.

Henri J.M. Nouwen[18]

The first week after the accident is a blur. After the first night, there was hardly time to think. Bad news travels quickly. For the first week, the phone didn't stop ringing. There were family, friends and others (some we knew well, others we hardly knew at all) visiting with flowers, meals, groceries, tears and kindness, shown in so many ways. Our home overflowed with floral tributes. There were calls to be made to those who didn't know yet. This was so difficult, so emotionally gut-wrenching.

The media called. Both the local Sutherland and Wollongong newspapers asked us for permission to print stories and photos. I agreed. I wanted the world to know that we had lost an angel. Our angel. I was (we all were) overwhelmed by people's love and concern for us. It did help. I felt carried along on an immense tidal wave of support. There was little time to be alone and process all that was happening, yet I only seemed to be able to cry when I was alone. When friends and family arrived, I put on my brave face. I usually need to be alone to experience sadness; otherwise, I feel the need to put on a show that I am coping okay. To tell the truth, I didn't know how I felt. I was in shock; I felt numb most of the time. Only people's kindness made it through my guard.

We were fortunate enough to have a friend who worked for Olsens Funerals. She was very kind to us and we were allowed to visit Simone in their mourning rooms as often as we liked. She also went to a lot of trouble to ensure that Simone's bruises and injuries were covered. Simone was dressed in the clothes we had chosen – yellow clothes, as this was her favourite colour.

While it was obviously Simone lying in the casket, it was merely her exterior, her shell. She was not there. It's not until you witness the body of someone you love, who has gone, that you appreciate the powerful element of the life force.

It was hard to connect with her, but I knew that this time was precious. We made the decision to bring all the kids with us, knowing that they needed a chance to say goodbye. I knew it was important for them to see her, to be able to acknowledge that she was really gone. It was such an unearthly experience – it was so real, yet so unreal at the same time. How do you prepare yourself and your children for an experience like that?

I was determined to speak at Simone's funeral. It wasn't hard to know what to talk about, there was so much to say. Choosing photos for the collage – celebrating all the ages and stages of her life – was difficult, we had so many photos to choose from. Choosing the music to play was harder still because music is such an emotive experience. It was clear to me that the songs needed to reflect both her taste in music and have lyrics that were important to her. I also wanted something special to accompany the photo collage. The music needed to be from one of her favourite Christian bands, but which one, and which song? She liked so many. I listened to many of her CDs, then one jumped out at me. It's called 'Tunnel', and is by the band Third Day.[19] It felt right on so many levels.

The musicians sing about the experience of being in a dark tunnel and how they want to bring their listeners light and hope. It seemed to me that it was written to provide comfort and a degree of optimism to those who are going through a hard time, who are perhaps depressed or even suicidal. But I also thought that they were words that would comfort us – all of us – family and congregation. There was light and hope for us, too, despite this terrible time of grief. It was also right on another level, one that most people present would not apprehend.

Simone had shared with me, on a number of occasions, her deep desire to go to heaven, to be with God. This wasn't always because she felt as though her life was too hard, although sometimes it was. It was more that she couldn't wait to go to heaven, and be with God forever. I found that really hard to hear. I wanted her to enjoy her life here, to enjoy being alive. And I remember telling her, 'There is so much you're living for,' just like in the words of this song.

Now I knew that Simone had reached that light at the end of her tunnel. She was with God, in the eternal light. I have kept this song on my iPod playlist. It makes me sad every time I hear it, of course, because it reminds me of losing Simone, as well as the experience of hearing this song during her funeral service. But I haven't deleted it because it is also good for me to be reminded that Simone has gone through her tunnel and into God's glorious light.

Another song, 'I Know You're There' by Casting Crowns,[20] was suggested by Simone's friend Erica, and the first time I heard it, I cried. I knew it was the right one. It gave me, and it still does, a strong visceral and emotional reaction. The lyrics speak about God being everywhere, that He hears us and is always there for us, wherever we are. It's a really beautiful song. Especially the words but also the melody. Again, this song felt right for a couple of reasons. Firstly, it gives hope to all of us, reminding us that our lives are not just sadness and grief, even now, because God is with us and around us. And, secondly, it confirmed what I knew in my heart of hearts – that Simone was with God, and also with me, and always would be. That gave me a sense of hope.

Public speaking has never been a problem for me, but speaking at your daughter's funeral is really tough. I felt that Simone deserved to have a mother who was strong enough to stand up and speak about her life. But I nearly didn't make it. Our close friend Sue had kindly offered to drive our family to the church and the cemetery. When we arrived, the church was overflowing. We were told that over three hundred people were attending the service. It was staggering. I saw our close family waiting in the front pews, struggling to hold it together. The photo collage we had chosen to highlight her life, accompanied by the music of Third Day, was playing. It felt overwhelming and painfully sad.

I was overcome by the number of friends, colleagues, teachers, students, acquaintances and families from our past – schools, workplaces, churches and others – who came to support us in our grief. I remember thinking to myself, *I hope Simone is seeing this. She would be so surprised to know how many people loved and cared for her.*

I was amazed at the impact Simone's life had had on those she had grown up alongside – her school, university and church friends, her teachers and students. And that so many people wanted to come, to remember Simone, celebrate her life and mourn her passing.

As I stood in the front row of the church that Simone had attended since she was two years old, I had visions of her running through my head – there was Simone, sitting in the front row during kids' story time. She was about two or three, and was constantly fiddling with her underwear, or her hair. Family times together at church, every Sunday, every Easter and Christmas. I remembered her Girls' Brigade parades, many years of them, when she stood beaming. I remembered her baptism as an adult when she made her proud confession of faith.

The next scene should clearly have been her wedding, not her funeral. Instead, there was a beautiful white coffin with a gorgeous arrangement of yellow and white native flowers, created by her friend Erica, who should have been the maid of honour at her wedding, not her funeral florist.

Nothing made sense.

How could someone like Simone be taken so soon, before she even had time to live her life? I had wanted – dreamed – of Simone falling in love, and getting married in this church. Yet here we were, at her funeral. I can't even speak of the service at the cemetery, where her body was taken for cremation. Letting her body go was the hardest thing I have ever had to do. I didn't want to let her go. At the last minute, in my mind, I was shouting, *Stop, no, I can't do this, I can't let her go*. But I just stood there mutely, reaching out to her imploringly with my arms, before collapsing into those of my father.

After the cemetery commitment ceremony, we went back to the church to meet the multitude of people who had come to support us that day. In the church hall, we had exhibited many of Simone's artworks – from university courses, Higher School Certificate and art studies, as well as her recreational pieces. It was a testament to Simone's gift as an artist to have them be acknowledged and admired. Many spoke of her artistic talent and all that she had achieved in her young life.

Naturally, it was an extremely emotional time: talking, crying and sharing memories with so many people, not only friends and connections of Simone's, but also colleagues from past and present workplaces, friends and volunteers from Lifeline, as well as friends and associates from our family life.

We came home, exhausted and drained, to a house replete with flower arrangements of every kind and design. Our life without Simone had begun.

CHAPTER 9

EARLY EXPERIENCES OF GRIEF

It was a time of paradoxes.

For the longest time, I felt curiously numb. Empty. My mind was in a complete fog, and I seemed unable to pierce the agony of my emotions with 'letting go' tears. To cry, I needed to look at photos of Simone or watch the video of the funeral. Otherwise, it didn't feel real, I didn't feel real. There was a huge hole inside me. A Simone-sized hole. And that was a very big hole to fill. While I understood intellectually that Simone was gone, it also felt as though there was a place inside me that was waiting for her to come home.

Everything was about Simone. I was reminded of her wherever I was, whatever was happening, whatever people were saying. Whenever I had any kind of random thought about her – a memory, experience, word or song – I would feel a physical jolt of pain. It could be triggered by anything: yellow (her favourite colour); a simple object such as a flower; an item of clothing or a car; hearing a song by one of her favourite bands; seeing one of her friends; hearing her name said out loud. Anything could do it. It felt as though a knife was twisting in my heart, or there was a cold churning in my guts or an icy trickle of fear.

This happened whenever I drew too close to the fact that it was real, that Simone not being here was really happening. I wanted to live in a bubble, in a world that didn't include the reality of Simone being gone.

For many years afterwards, I felt this weird internal struggle – I knew that Simone had gone, but I also found it really hard to believe. A lingering sense of unreality persisted, as if I were living in an alternate version of reality. I now know that grief can make you feel like you are going crazy. And that this is entirely normal.

The hardest and most painful part to live with was the physical longing – an unbridled yearning – for Simone. In the initial days and weeks, but also as weeks became months, and months became years, my desire to see, touch, hold, hug, kiss and experience Simone's presence was physically painful. My arms ached to hold her; my eyes needed to see her; I longed to stroke her beautiful golden hair. I wanted to feel her presence, to look into her eyes, to experience her smile. I needed to hear her voice, her stories, and for her to be part of our family. The cold reality of death is so hard, so final. I wanted to resist the reality of her not being here, but each day dawned and Simone did not come back home to us.

At home, Simone's place at the table was empty. It was so quiet, and so strange, to live life without her. Our dinner table felt stark and awkward. Our family felt so small. Just the five of us. It was hard for us to know how to sit around the table. Simone always sat in the same spot, opposite Laura, and they would often play games and footsies under the table. Laura could no longer sit in her spot, it was too difficult for her, so we kept changing places around the table.

I remember sitting out on our leafy deck for dinner, surrounded by the soaring Sydney red gums. I usually take so much comfort from them, yet all I could see was that empty space at the outdoor table, where Simone should be. I sifted through memories, trying to visualise her sitting there. But it brought no peace. It didn't matter where we set up for dinner – out on the deck, in our dining room or at our smaller breakfast nook – we couldn't avoid that empty space. I would try to grasp memories of our last dinner times with Simone, to hold on to a sense of her presence with us. I was conscious of Simone not being with us all the time. Our family felt incomplete without her. Our previous habit of having long conversations at the dinner table ended; it felt uncomfortable sitting for long at our table, as it emphasised Simone's absence.

Simone was such a big character in our family. She had brought so much passion and presence into our family, and family life felt diminished: smaller, quieter. The family dynamic had totally flipped. Daniel, the quiet, introverted child, was the eldest now; he had no experience in that role, as the leader of the kids. I had always thought that a family of six was so big, four kids was a lot. Now I couldn't believe how small our family was. I wanted my big, noisy family back.

Tony and I both struggled with guilt. Our most important job as parents had been to protect Simone, to keep her safe and alive, and we had failed in our responsibility. I blamed myself, because I had argued with her the night before, and sent her to bed before she was ready. This, I reasoned, had led to her being tired and not focusing on driving as well as she could have. *If I had just left her alone … If I had just left her to decide when to go to bed, she may have slept better and then … if she had slept better then she wouldn't have been so tired and then …* and *Why was I so obsessed about her finishing that bloody assignment – it never even mattered in the end.* So many 'if onlys' and 'should haves'.

Beyond the guilt, I felt shame and a deep sense of regret that the final two conversations I'd had with Simone were angry ones. My last words, my last experience of her was overshadowed by these dark, negative feelings. These were not the memories that I wanted Simone to remember me by. I hate that my final memory of Simone is tainted by my anger and frustration. This was not the way I wanted to say my final goodbye.

Tony blamed himself for Simone's car having a fault in the muffler. The night before the accident Simone had complained of the muffler being noisy, so Tony had put a bandage on it, a temporary measure until the weekend when he would have time to repair it properly.

His 'if onlys' and 'should haves' were *If only I had fixed the muffler straight away, the car wouldn't have been so noisy. Maybe she had the music on loud because the muffler was noisy, so she wasn't concentrating properly ...* and *If she had a different car, one without a driver's seat so close to the engine, then she wouldn't have been killed in the accident. I should have let her take my car that day.* We tortured ourselves with guilt, which only succeeded in making us feel worse.

A lot of people feel angry when confronted with loss. They may feel intense anger towards the person who died, for leaving them. Or they may direct their anger onto someone else related to the person they lost – the driver of the vehicle who killed them, the loved one's partner, the illness, society in large, the universe. Or God. Whomever they see as to blame, either directly for the loss, or someone who let them down.

The anger I experienced, however, was directed largely towards myself, for not having been able to change or fix my relationship with Simone before she died. I felt no anger whatsoever towards Simone. How could I be angry with Simone now? It was an accident. There was no way that I could feel anger towards her – and I had wasted enough time and energy on anger. I felt only sorrow and distress, about how much fear, pain and suffering she may have experienced in those last moments of life. And tenderness and sadness, that she had lost her life so young, and would never experience the ongoing joys of life. But no anger, not at Simone.

I did feel angry at people who said that Simone had died for a reason, that Simone's life was a testimony for faith. Or those who said that people would be challenged by her death and realise that they should make their peace with God. Or hearing that there were people in the traffic jam (in the wake of Simone's accident) who were approached by other Christians during the wait, and this may have saved a soul. Or that Simone was too good for this world. Or that only the good die young. Or that Tony and I were strong enough to handle this loss. People intended to be encouraging, but none of this was helpful.

The best thing people could do was cry with me, feel with me, be sad with me, agree with me about the injustice of her death – that meant a lot. Greeting-card sentiments did nothing. They felt abrasive, and simply rubbed more salt into our wounds.

To be quite honest, I didn't care about other people being brought to faith through Simone's death. It may sound like a nice and peachy sentiment; unless, that is, you are the mother of the child who has died. I could never believe or accept this idea, and I did not want Simone to be the reason for people to be saved. Call me selfish, but I just wanted Simone. I wanted her alive. She could save more souls that way. Whenever people spoke or wrote to me about these notions, I would inwardly shout or groan, though I kept my thoughts to myself.

I have felt angry at God, but not in a loud-and-shouting kind of way. Angry in a sad, disillusioned, desperate kind of way. How many times had I asked God to look after her, to keep her safe? It was my prayer every morning and every night. I don't believe that God caused Simone's accident because I don't think He works that way, but I did think that He could have saved her, that she could have been injured, or been in a temporary coma and ultimately lived. These faith concerns have been part of an ongoing struggle that I am continuing to work through.

For a long time, I could not and would not take part in the pastimes that I used to enjoy, such as reading, or listening to music, or watching television or enjoying food. I normally love to eat, and am somewhat of a comfort eater, but nice food held no appeal, for a long time. I am an avid reader but, for the greater part of a year, I had no desire to read. It was a strange mixture of apathy and guilt. Apathy, because I couldn't really care about anything; guilt, because Simone could no longer enjoy these things, so why should I? I know that Tony struggled in a similar way, and for even longer than I did. Sometime during that first year, I slowly started to pick up these hobbies again. Too much time to think and dwell is not good when you are prone to anxiety and depression.

In those first difficult days and weeks after we lost Simone, I was also desperately waiting and anticipating that Simone would reach out to me, to speak or connect with me in some way. That may sound as though I'm crazy. However, due to prior experiences of loss, and due to reading about people who've had near-death experiences, I knew that it was possible for Simone to come to me, either in a dream, a vision or as a spiritual presence. I didn't know how or when it would happen, but I was waiting. I was waiting and hoping and expecting it to happen, somewhat impatiently. I thought that maybe I was being punished for not being a good enough mother.

My daughter Laura had a dream on the night of the accident, where Simone spoke to her and told her to 'go on without her'. I didn't have any dreams like that. I begged, I pleaded with Simone, and with God, to talk to me, to come to me. I hoped she would tell me she loved me, tell me that she forgave me. I did that for many years, not just in the early days. Nothing happened.

I did have one curious experience, however. It was a few days before the funeral and some of my closest friends were sitting with me on our deck, talking and praying. There was a dragonfly that kept flying around the table, and then flying around me. It perched on my shoulder, and it stayed there for what seemed like a few minutes. Then it landed on my arm for a minute or so. Then it perched on the table, directly in front of me. It hovered and flew around me. The experience lasted for about five minutes, maybe more. My friend Anne, who was sitting next to me, looked at me and said, 'Are you thinking what I'm thinking?' Yes, I most certainly was. Wishful thinking? Perhaps. Maybe it was just a curious trick of nature, but I've had a soft spot for dragonflies ever since.

Every September, dragonflies gather around my front door and hover around me. I have been known to creep down our front stairway and sit with them. I particularly look out for yellow ones.

Do I believe that Simone inhabits a dragonfly? No, but could they be a messenger of hope? Possibly. Apparently, dragonflies have long been associated with those who are grieving. I came across a number of websites that referenced the presence of dragonflies around those who have lost a loved one. And there was a common theme among the websites that dragonflies are symbolic, representing 'the souls of departed loved ones returned to Earth to reassure their loved ones that they're doing okay in the afterlife'.[21] The aquatic entomologist who wrote this also stated that many people had contacted her about their experiences with dragonflies after the death of a loved one. As a scientist, she was sceptical, but she'd had her own experience of visits by dragonflies after the loss of her father.

For Laura, the presence of a kookaburra is what she finds comforting, perceiving it to be symbolic of Simone's presence. Experiences with animals or birds are also mentioned in literature and websites that discuss experiences with the deceased.

There were other experiences, too. A client at Anglicare, who said that she 'saw things at times', told me that she had seen the image of a young girl with long blonde hair in a yellow knitted jumper hovering around my head when I was counselling her. She had been embarrassed to tell me, but I was delighted. Simone had a favourite yellow knitted jumper when she was about ten.

My friend Ruth told me a story about six months after Simone's death. She was awkward and uncomfortable about it, but she wanted to tell me of an experience she had on the night of Simone's funeral. I was very open to hear what she had to say. Ruth, as well as being a good friend of mine, was also close to Simone. For a time, they were joint leaders of a girls' Bible-study group. At the time of the funeral, Ruth and her family were away on holiday and were unable to attend the funeral. Ruth told me that she felt very sad and conflicted about not having been able to attend. That night, she was restless. Lying in a strange hotel room, she noticed that there was a light in the room. Confused, she looked around, trying to find the source. She looked at her husband sleeping beside her and was shocked to see a young girl who looked like Simone, but at a much younger age, perhaps around ten or twelve, hovering around his head. Ruth told me that she looked very peaceful and content.

I was caught in a state of emotional turmoil. While I was delighted to hear this story, I also felt sad and disappointed. Why had Simone come to visit Ruth and not me? What had stopped or prevented Simone from appearing to me? In a sense, it was crushing to hear, but to learn that Simone was around and was peaceful and content was also very comforting.

CHAPTER 10

THE CHALLENGES OF GRIEF

In the early weeks and months, when I was round and about – in the supermarket or shopping centre – I observed that some people would deliberately avoid me. I would catch them looking down or darting down an aisle to evade me. And, sometimes, it would be me doing the evading – if I was having a bad day and I didn't want to talk about Simone. Many times, I would have the feeling (whether they avoided me or not) that when people saw me, they thought of me as 'that poor woman who lost her daughter in a car accident'. As though that was my new identity. I didn't like the idea at all.

There were so many challenges that year. Being a year of firsts, it was always going to be difficult. Although my life felt like it had stopped, life's demands continued to make their claims upon us. We still had a family who needed us. A few short weeks after the funeral, Daniel had his end-of-school awards assembly and then his year 12 formal. We couldn't let these events pass by without taking part and making Daniel feel just as special and important as his sister was when she went through these landmark events. So, we put our brave faces on and went out there and did it.

Then there were the Higher School Certificate exams. We needed to support Daniel as he tried to study in the wake of the huge loss of his sister. Laura was completing her first year at high school, and Matt was in year 4 at primary school. There were more awards ceremonies and end-of-year events.

The challenges kept coming. The first big one was collecting Simone's ashes from the cemetery. After some discussion, Tony and I decided that we wouldn't place Simone's ashes in the cemetery. That didn't feel right to us at all. The cemetery was too far away. And it was probably too much of a reality hit for us to face back then. We didn't want Simone to be in the cemetery, far away from us, we wanted her with us, at home. So, we decided to place her ashes in a beautiful rosewood box, and keep her in the heart of her family, where she belonged. We chose a picture of Simone to place on the front face of the box. It was a photo that we both loved. It was taken on our last family day out, on Father's Day, three days before she died. Simone is on the ferry, directly facing the photographer (Tony), and she looks peaceful and calm.

The cemetery called to let me know that the box with the ashes was ready to be picked up. It was a few months after the funeral, so it took me by surprise when the call finally came. I foolishly decided to go on my own, having no idea how monumental this task would be. I was okay until I had to put Simone in the car. I didn't know how best to place her. I couldn't put her in the boot, like some parcel. And she couldn't be a back-seat passenger. I decided to put her in the front passenger seat and I fastened her in carefully, with a seatbelt. It was bizarre. *How do I do this? How do I take what is left of Simone home?* There were no instructions. I slowly made my way out of the cemetery, feeling like a mother taking her baby on a drive for the first time. But this was my dead baby. My eyes blurred; the tears rained down, as my heart hammered, seeking to break out of my chest. I had to stop the car and pull myself together. *Why*, I asked myself, *did I not think to wait for Tony to come with me, or ask a friend to help me? Should I go back, and come back another time? No, no. That's silly. They will think I am silly. I just have to do it.*

It was a slow and difficult drive home. The cemetery is only fifteen minutes away from home, but the trip felt twice as long that day. When I arrived home, I was exhausted. Later, when I told friends and colleagues what I had done, they were shocked that I hadn't thought to ask someone to accompany me on such a symbolic journey. It just hadn't occurred to me. My mother had taught me to be strong and independent, and not to rely on others, so I just did what had to be done. Dutch stoicism in action.

Next, was the challenge of what to do with Simone's bedroom. I felt as though I couldn't do anything with Simone's room and belongings. I didn't want to erase any of the memories that she had left behind. For a long time, I left her room exactly the way she had left it. It was a mess, but it didn't feel right to change it. Tony and the kids were also not ready for anything to be changed.

However, after a while, with my family's permission, I tidied her room just enough for me to feel comfortable, without losing the essence of who Simone was. It was comforting to be there, to feel close to Simone. I would sit on her bed, look through her dresses, her favourite clothes, hold them and breathe in any leftover scent of her. I would remember how she loved her pink woollen beanie, her red leather wallet, her favourite green hoodie that she wore all the time and her painting jeans. I would read through her books and journals, and I tried to decipher some of the hundred or so scrawled bits of paper around her room. I would absorb being in her room, almost as though I was trying to breathe her in, to physically feel her presence with me. Sometimes it worked. More often, it didn't. I would look through her photos and try to track back memories of a lifetime of moments spent with Simone. The memories were mixed, bittersweet. Many brought a smile to my face; others were harder to face. Sharp. Heavy. Forlorn.

One piece of writing that was particularly poignant was Simone's plan – her run sheet, you could say – for the day she died. We found it in the bag she took to uni that day. Her blue library bag, filled with fragments of glass from the smashed front window of her car. As with many of her notes, the writing was difficult to decipher. What was agonising to see was how she had even itemised the drive home that day from uni: '5.30 – 7pm drive home'. There were also reminder notes: 'work out proper real handout'; 'handout draft to consider while driving (no music)'; 'drawing'; 'plan explanation alteration, consider while driving home'; 'adjust worksheet'. The sense I made from this was that she had a lot on her mind that day, and perhaps she wasn't focusing clearly on the road or the truck. This was one of many theories I had – they jostled in mind as I tried to make meaning of how the accident happened.

Another note that raised complicated feelings was the one that Simone left for us on the day she died. This was not unusual, because she would often leave some scribbled instructions or information that we or she needed to know. On one side, the note said, 'To Dad' in big letters, and 'or Mum' in smaller letters (as the note was really meant for Tony to act on).

Gonna need extra petrol money 2 get 2 oak flats +
Money 4 printing @ uni today (cos I can't at home)

To print my assignment in colour. Which I
REALLY REALLY need.
I need 2
A print it at Uni ($1 a page) ($10 total) which will take ages
Or B
We need black ink 4 home
If you prefer B can you PLEASE get black ink TOMORROW
or if you can't because it would be very difficult 4 me 2 get tomorrow.
Plz leave a message (or I'll ring You)
♥ SiM_onE

There was also a multitude of scribbled prayers about the cares of her heart. I felt like an intruder reading these rambling thoughts and concerns but, simultaneously, I felt justified because I could no longer speak to Simone about these things. They were the only tangible bits of Simone that I had left. As it was, most of what she wrote was impossible to decipher. What I did gain was a sense of the depth of her faith and trust in God. And I learned more about one particular young man she had given her heart to, who didn't return her love. I knew about this unfulfilled dream of her heart, and it hurt me that she experienced this anguish. And it now hurts whenever I see him. It causes a burning physical ache in my heart. Because when I see him, I remember Simone and how he didn't love her as she loved him.

Somehow, time passed, much of it a blur. After a couple of months, I decided to go back to work. I was hoping that focusing on other people's problems would take my mind off my own. In retrospect, it was too early, but I didn't really understand that till sometime later. It was traumatising to pass the accident site. As I worked in Wollongong three days a week, I would need to pass the place on Mount Ousley Road where the accident occurred. For a long time, I couldn't pass the accident site without experiencing some kind of physical pain – an icy twist in my gut, a dizziness in my head or a sharp pain in my chest. Often, I would find myself involuntarily reliving the day of the accident. I would imagine what Simone was thinking and feeling as she was driving that day.

I wondered whether she saw the truck she was about to crash into, and I hoped to God that she hadn't. I couldn't allow my mind to dwell on the physical and emotional pain Simone would have experienced when the collision occurred. That was far too real, too awful. Instead, I would picture the long line of traffic that was waiting for the police and ambulance to attend the scene that evening, and then for the site to be cleared. I would try to prepare myself in advance for that slow incline up the hill, to the place where my beautiful Simone had died.

People have said to me that they didn't know how I did it, that they wouldn't have been able to. But it's amazing what you can do when you feel that you have no choice. In my mind, I had to go to work, so I had to go past the accident site. There was an alternative route that I could have taken, which was suggested to me by a few people. This route would add an extra fifteen minutes to what was already a fifty-minute journey. To me, this addition of time meant changing my trip wasn't justified. I thought that I would just have to 'be strong', as my mother taught me to be. 'You have to grow up, Connie, and be strong. The world is a tough place.' So, I toughened up and I was strong.

It was my idea to place a marker at the accident site. After travelling past it so many times, I needed a focal point that marked the tragedy that had occurred here. As we didn't have a site at the cemetery, a physical place that represented Simone and our loss, it felt really important for us to remember Simone and the accident that took her life in this way, and also for others to know that something significant had happened here.

We decided on a small white wooden cross, to which we attached a stainless-steel engraved plaque. The words we decided to place on the plaque were:

SiM_onE
Simone Maree Easterbrook
17th March 1987 – 10th September 2008
A gifted artist, a much-loved daughter, sister and granddaughter
A passionate and committed ambassador for Christ
Her life ended here but the memories are eternal ones

SiM_onE was Simone's logo from her graphic arts days, and the way that she would often sign her messages, written or text. The capital letters were to represent her initials, S.M.E. Another, similar plaque was placed at the University of Wollongong, upon their invitation. The university contacted us to explain their idea of holding a service for Simone's fellow students, friends and staff, to commemorate Simone's life and plant a tree and place marker in her honour. This informal service was held two months after Simone died and was presided over by the university's Evangelical Union pastor, who knew Simone through her involvement with their activities. A few of Simone's friends and fellow students who also spoke about her. The tree was then planted and the plaque erected. Our whole family was invited, and the education faculty lecturers invited us to have lunch with them at one of the university cafes. It was very moving to be supported by the university in this way and I will never forget their thoughtfulness.

We were extremely impressed by the university's care and support for our family. In addition to the service and an official condolence letter from the dean, we received gift baskets from the staff and fellow students in the education faculty, including a huge poster containing personal messages. There were also multiple Facebook posts and email messages of support. The university administrators also went above and beyond to help Daniel gain enrolment in his chosen Bachelor of Arts programme.

The ultimate sign of their care, however, was the official graduation ceremony for the education students, to which our family and Simone's friends were invited to attend. Simone was posthumously awarded her Graduate Diploma in Education. When Tony and I went onto the stage to accept Simone's award, with great trepidation and nervousness, we were greeted with a standing ovation and applause that seemed to last forever. It was a very emotional and powerful experience. I trust that Simone was there with us, feeling proud that she had achieved her goal and this amazing honour. This was an experience I will never forget. (It still gives me goosebumps whenever I remember it.)

The next challenge was our first Christmas without Simone. I really didn't want to celebrate Christmas at all that year. To be honest, since the loss of my mother at Christmas two years earlier, I had dreaded Christmas. Now, there were two losses to bear, and they fell heavily on us. But we felt it would be unfair on our children to not celebrate Christmas, so we did the best we could.

Our extended family was very loving and thoughtful. My gorgeous brother-in-law was so kind and caring. He didn't say much, but I knew by his hug, the expression in his eyes and his few short words that he knew exactly how I was feeling. He had lost his father to lung cancer shortly after we lost Simone, so he had a genuine sense of how we were feeling.

The next big challenge was Simone's birthday, in March, six months after the accident. The build-up was particularly stressful, worrying about how we were going to get through the day. I thought it would be good to bring all the family together and go to one of Simone's favourite places to eat, a German restaurant in Beverly Hills. We wanted the day to be a celebration of Simone, rather than focusing on her death. It was a memorable night, and it did help us to make it through the complexities and strains of that first birthday.

What took me by surprise was our first Easter without Simone, shortly after her birthday. We arrived at the packed church service and took our seats in the upper balcony. I looked around at all the families present. All the *complete* families. It seemed as though everyone had gathered their family together to celebrate Easter. Everyone except us. I remembered how much Simone loved Easter. She had always enjoyed it more than Christmas. She loved the Easter egg hunt, as she was a passionate lover of all things chocolate. I remembered other Easter services that we had all attended together. I started to feel hot and teary, and I had to leave. I couldn't stay. I wasn't able to focus on the service anyway. I think what made this experience so hard was that I hadn't psychologically prepared myself for it. If I know that there is going to be a triggering event, I brace myself emotionally. I hadn't anticipated that Easter would be as hard as it was.

For me, the most difficult experience of that devastating year was the anticipation of the first anniversary of her death. What was uncanny was that my body knew that the day was approaching before my mind did. I was driving to work one day, I think it was late July, about six weeks before 10 September. Suddenly, I started to feel very upset and sad, but it was a strange sort of sadness that seemed to seep out from my flesh and bones. No thoughts preceded these emotions. It was a very strange experience, like nothing I had ever felt before.

I noticed that every song I heard seemed to be about Simone. I thought to myself, *I cannot go to work today.* But my strong sense of conscientiousness said otherwise, replying, *Don't be silly. Today is just like any other day. You are nearly there. Go to work. You will be fine once you get there.* But I wasn't fine. Tears started raining down, uninvited. I told the receptionist that I didn't think I was ready for my first client and asked if she could make my apologies, which she did.

Then, fortunately, my dear friend and colleague Eileen came in to see me. She was the psychologist that I had seen all those years ago, when Simone was three and I was struggling with postnatal depression. She understood me like no one else and her loving support was just what I needed. After much hugging, love and prayer, she sent me home.

The next six weeks were extremely difficult, and I started to dread the day. I decided that we needed to do something special, something that was all about Simone. We started the day by going to the accident site and university, and laying flowers in memory of Simone. Then we went to the beach and placed yellow flowers in the waves, because Simone loved the beach. This ended up being a joyous event because we brought our lovable Labrador, Oscar, and he had a great time frolicking in the waves. It was good that we were able to laugh, even though we felt so sad.

In the evening, we invited family, close friends and all those who had a special connection with Simone, to celebrate her life at our place. There were about twenty people present. We crowded into our lounge room in a large circle, and I invited everyone to share a special memory about Simone. There was laughter and tears. I shared a few of my special moments and most of the others did, too. Then we had supper, with all of Simone's favourites – ice-cream cones, lollies and chocolate. Simone would have loved it! The day itself was a lot easier than I had thought it would be.

The anticipation had been the hardest part. Making a time to remember Simone, to share happy, unique and special experiences made it a celebration, instead of only a day of mourning.

Every birthday and every anniversary since, we go to the accident site and the commemoration tree at the University of Wollongong. We start our day by going to the florist, choosing some yellow flowers – roses, dahlias or sunflowers – and we drive to the accident site and secure them to the cross. Then we spend a few minutes in silence, reflecting on Simone and her life and our loss. It is an important ritual for all of us, and it helps to keep Simone's memory alive. For the first few years all the kids came with us, and sometimes Tony's parents would come along. More recently, it has usually just been Tony and me.

Rituals are very important in grief. That is why funerals are so important and healing. It is a public acknowledgement of loss and recognises the importance of the person who died to those left behind. While I still find it comforting to follow this ritual on the anniversary of Simone's death, over time I have found it difficult on Simone's birthday. It doesn't feel quite right to me to be carrying out this sad and difficult task on a day when I would prefer to be celebrating her life. However, I have kept the ritual going for Tony's sake. It is important to him to continue it, so I have maintained it for his benefit. And a part of me does feel that if we didn't continue to remember her in this way it might feel as though her memory had become less important over time, and that we were somehow failing in our commitment to keeping her memory alive in our hearts.

I have other, personal rituals that I follow, either on her anniversary or her birthday. I spend part of the day looking at photos, or reading some of her favourite books or journals she has written, or I sit quietly and reflect about Simone. I usually talk to her, too.

During the first couple of years, at 6.20 pm (the time of the accident) on the anniversary of her death, our family would join hands and sit for a few moments in silence to remember Simone. Then we'd pray or share our thoughts and memories. It was a very sacred time, a ritual of connection and healing.

For the first five years or so, our family – our parents, siblings and their families, along with our immediate family – went out for lunch or dinner on Simone's birthday to enjoy the kind of meal Simone loved. This would be Japanese, Chinese, yum cha or a schnitzel restaurant. On the anniversary of her loss we would often go to the beach, a place she loved, to remember Simone.

It is now nearly fourteen years since Simone died. (I have been writing this book over the past five years.) Her birthday and death day continue to be difficult. Both days feel overshadowed by an inner sense of darkness and sadness. I have learnt that it is best not to go to work on the anniversary of her loss. In earlier years I tried, once or twice, to go if her birthday fell on a workday, but I ended up being triggered by my work, and I would need to leave early. Perhaps it would be easier if my work didn't focus on people's emotional and/or family experiences. But it does. I have now tentatively begun to work on her birthday, but continue to find it difficult to work on the anniversary of her loss. I also want to honour her death day by not working. So does Tony.

Above: My four cheeky munchkins. Simone thought it would be fun for each of them to wear an orange T-shirt for a family photo, displaying their varying heights. This was Mum's favourite photo of her grandchildren.

Top right: Dress ups for a youth group activity: Simone (16), Laura (8), Matthew (4). Simone is wearing her year 10 formal dress and tiara.

All four kids with our first family dog, a boxer called Roxy.

Simone's 18th birthday celebration with friends from school and youth group, at a Chinese restaurant at Engadine.

Simone (18), Laura (10) at Cockington Green, Canberra, 2005.

Family photo taken in my sister-in-law's backyard. Simone (19), Daniel (16), Laura (11), Matthew (7).

Family dinner on our deck on Simone's actual 21st birthday. This photo clearly demonstrates the strong, loving bonds between Simone and her siblings.

Simone and Daniel at her 21st birthday party. The theme was 'ancient times'. Simone in 'ancient' Japanese dress, Daniel in 'caveman' dress.

Family Christmas, 2007, the year after Mum died. Simone and Daniel are reliving a family joke.

Simone, on the ferry to the Biennale with her dad. This is the photo we placed on the rosewood box containing her ashes.

Simone, Laura and me, on the ferry to the Biennale, three days before Simone's fatal car accident.

This is approximately where the accident happened, on Mount Ousley Road, Bellambi.

A close-up of the memorial we placed at the side of the road, Mount Ousley Road, Bellambi.

SiM_onE
Simone Maree Easterbrook
17th March 1987 - 10th September 2008

The article in the *Illawarra Mercury* following Simone's accident. A similar article was in the *St George and Sutherland Shire Leader*.

A passionate life

Crash victim's dream was to be a teacher

By JODIE MINUS

SIMONE Easterbrook was a passionate, persistent young woman and the eldest child of four in a tight-knit Sutherland family.

Quietly spoken and a little bit shy to the outside world, within the love of her family she was bubbly, excitable and outgoing, with dreams of becoming a school teacher.

But those dreams came to a sad end on Wednesday evening when Ms Easterbrook, 21, was tragically killed in a car accident on Mt Ousley Rd.

Yesterday, Ms Easterbrook's devastated parents Anthony and Connie and siblings Daniel, 18, Laura, 13, and Matthew, 9, were at their Woronora Heights home seeking comfort in their Christian faith as they struggle with their loss.

"We are all together and we have a lot of love and support from the church community," Mrs Easterbrook said.

"Last night was very shocking but today we have been getting a lot of calls from family and friends and we are with family now.

"We are devastated, just devastated and just wondering now how we are going to come to terms with it."

Ms Easterbrook was a self-described "Shire girl" who had lived in the region all her life. She attended West Engadine Public School and Heathcote High School before studying Visual Arts at the University of Wollongong. After graduating in 2007, she continued to study for her graduate diploma of education.

Born into the Christian faith, Ms Easterbrook attended services at the Heathcote Engadine Baptist Church and had spent a few summers volunteering her time at Huskisson Beach Mission, a holiday children's outreach centre.

In her spare time she honed her painting and portraiture talents and also loved relaxing at the beach.

"She loved the warm weather and she loved the beach," Mrs Easterbrook said.

A date has not yet been set for Ms Easterbrook's funeral.

Killed: Simone at her 21st birthday. Her family is devastated by her death.

Study days: Simone Easterbrook was finishing her Diploma in Education after graduating last year in Visual Arts from the University of Wollongong.

My brother Danny, aged 27, a few months before he died.

My mother Will, aged 73, taken a few months before she died.

The memory box I created at a grief seminar.

CHAPTER 11

LIFE IS WHAT HAPPENS ...

Before Simone's death, I had already experienced two significant losses, and they'd had a great impact on my life. All three experiences have shaped my understanding about the diverse ways grief and loss affect our lives.

I had two brothers, John and Danny. My brother John is a shy and quiet guy, a bit of a dreamer. John admits that he probably fits the criteria for inattentive ADHD, but he has never felt the need to be diagnosed. He was a daydreamer at school, always zoning out and looking out the window. Being inattentive, rather than hyperactive, however, he escaped the attention given to the more obvious (loud) problem behaviours of some fellow students, who screamed ADHD. John now works as a pattern maker, a form of carpentry. He is an amazing craftsman and builder. He built his own house on the South Coast, and then went on to renovate a unit and another three houses. John, following in the family footsteps, is a perfectionist and he has excelled in all his building works. Actually, in every project or hobby he puts his mind to. I am in awe of his gifts.

My brother Danny hadn't really found his calling in the early 1990s. He'd first worked at a bakery and was considering a career as a chef. Then he moved into retail. When he was in his early twenties, he really wanted to join the church ministry but, due to his tender age, our minister suggested that he gain some life experience first. So, he began a career in banking, biding his time. Danny was a hard worker, highly regarded by his managers, and soon he was promoted to the position of personal lender. Danny was very loyal and committed to his job, and wouldn't tolerate any negative comments about his employer (the Commonwealth Bank). Danny had a strong faith in God, and I was inspired and proud of his profound spiritual convictions. The two of us often discussed issues of faith and life. He also preached voluntarily at local churches.

When Danny was nearly twenty-one, he married his teenage sweetheart Tania. It was a beautiful wedding. It was very special for us because Simone was invited to be the flower girl, aged nearly three. She was gorgeous! We had some fears about how she would behave, as she was very boisterous during the practice session but, on the day, she behaved beautifully. She was so overwhelmed by the people and the excitement that she was very quiet, which was both a surprise and a relief.

I always enjoyed Danny's company, even though I was often the butt of his joking and clowning around. Danny, the third child, was the clown of the family, which is described by psychologists as typical of the third-born. He loved to play practical jokes on his friends and family, and no one was exempt from his quirky sense of humour. He used to ring me and pretend to be a crank caller of some description, or a bank official telling me I was overdrawn on my account. He was rarely serious. It was hard work trying to maintain a sane conversation with him most of the time. Danny was a good looking and intelligent guy who, I thought, had so much going for him.

As Danny and Tania lived nearby, we used to see a lot of them. Danny loved being an uncle to his two young nieces and nephew. They had a swimming pool, so we often dropped in so the kids could enjoy it. However, soon after Laura was born, to our great shock, Danny told us that he and Tania were separating, offering no explanation about why. They had been married for about five years. As a family, we were all very sad and confused. About a year later, we had a family celebration for Laura's first birthday and, a few weeks later, Daniel's sixth birthday. Danny couldn't make it to Daniel's family celebration, so he came over a few days later and spent the afternoon playing Lego with Daniel, while I tidied the house (as usual).

Two weeks later, I received an urgent request to call my mother. It had been one of those days you sometimes have with three young children. I was running around all day – to and from school, visiting parents, doing shopping, after-school activities. A friend at the school told me that my parents had rung her trying to get in touch with me and for me to call them. This was in the days before I had a mobile phone. I wasn't too disturbed, as I had seen my parents a few hours before and I assumed that they wanted to tell me that my mother had been able to secure a time for her surgery (as we had talked about it that day). However, my friend was insistent that I call my mother straight away. I tried calling from her house, but the line was engaged, so I proceeded to take Simone to her jazz ballet class.

While the lesson was on, I took Laura and Daniel around the shops. Then I decided to try calling my mother from a payphone at the local shopping centre. For years afterwards, I couldn't walk past that phone without remembering the trauma of that call. My mother told me, over the phone, that Danny had died. As I was standing there, alone, with two young children, I discovered that my brother had taken his own life the night before. I remember shouting, screaming and crying all at once. People around were staring at me like I was crazy. I saw them, but I didn't discern them. The world around me blurred and whirled. No one should receive news like that, alone in a public phone box.

Somehow, I made my way back to the jazz ballet studio, collected Simone with some stumbled explanation and drove home. I remember my mind was shouting at me, *This can't be true, not my brother, not Danny.* I was in a complete daze; it felt so surreal and horrifying. I don't know, to this day, how I made it home safely with three kids. I kept telling myself that it couldn't be true, that this could not have happened – to him, to me, to our family.

I rang Tony as soon as I reached the house. I simply told him that something terrible had happened and that I needed him to come home, straight away. My voice must have sounded very shaky and shocked. Poor Tony. He told me days later that because I didn't tell him what the terrible news was, he didn't know what to expect when he arrived home. He said that his mind had raced to the fearful conclusion that something had happened to one of our children. It was a nightmare trip home for him. I'm not sure why I didn't tell him; I guess that I didn't want to shock him the way my mother had shocked me by telling me such horrific news over the phone. However, in retrospect, I realise that I should have at least told him that the kids were safe. It didn't occur to me at the time that this would be a natural fear for him. When something this shocking, this unexpected, happens, your brain just doesn't work. I was in total shock. My mind could not take it in. It seemed to take forever for Tony to come home and, somehow, I had to explain to the children why their mother was behaving so strangely. I can't remember now what I told them. I think it was that I'd just had some bad news, but I knew one thing that I was not going to tell them. And that was how their uncle had died.

After Tony had arrived and I explained what had happened, we took the kids to my in-laws and drove to my parents' home. This was a horrific scene. Mum and Dad were in a shocked and dishevelled state, my brother John was there, the minister from their church, the minister from our church, and a few of Mum's closest friends. I remember leaving that night and fearing for my own sanity. I was already struggling with depression, and I had no idea about how I could or would cope.

I have one clear memory from the morning after I learned of my brother's death. It was a beautiful sunny day – the sky was a clear, vibrant blue. Yet this felt like an affront to me. How dare the sun keep shining when my brother was no longer living? The words from the Wendy Matthews song 'The Day You Went Away'[22] have resonated with me since, as she sings about the cloudless blue sky on a day when the world should be rainy and dismal.

As I hung the clothes on the line, I remember thinking and praying, *God, Danny has died, he's taken his own life, and yet here I am still – living, breathing, hanging the clothes on the line, just like any other ordinary day. And the sky is still blue.*

Somehow, though, the fact that I hadn't died or gone crazy during the night seemed to persuade me that I could survive this. It felt shocking in one way, but comforting at the same time. I remember thinking that if I could live even one day through the pain of something so huge – still live and breathe, still do those everyday life things – then I would be okay. I think that knowing this helped to prepare me for the days ahead.

Bereavement by suicide is one of those experiences that you don't expect to touch you personally. It happens out there, to other families, dysfunctional families. Not to my normal, ordinary kind of family. My brother's suicide led to me feeling, all of a sudden, that the world didn't make sense. It was as though the Earth had tilted on its axis, and I couldn't understand it in the same way that I had before. Whenever I reflect back on my life, I remember this as a turning point, a crossroads in my life. I would never think about life in quite the same way again. And I know that others who've experienced loss through suicide have had similar experiences.

One of the distinctive aspects of suicide grief is that the 'why' question is asked over and over again. It's part of the reason that grieving a suicide is so complicated. The overpowering need to know why is intensified. Like others bereaved by suicide, I became preoccupied by the why question. There were so many unanswered and unanswerable questions – my brother was happy, so, how and why could he do this? Why didn't he tell me, or anyone else in the family, how he was feeling? Why suicide? I was plagued by guilt, thinking what a bad sister I was for not knowing, for not asking, for not taking the time to find out how Danny was feeling after the collapse of his marriage. And I was studying psychology at that time – surely, I should have known. What sort of psychologist would I become if I didn't know that my own brother was hurting so much?

I remembered, too late, that there was a time when I had talked to Danny about some questions I was having about my faith. He had sadly responded that he didn't have the answers anymore, that he couldn't help me because he was struggling with his own demons. The conversation had saddened me because it was so different to what I'd experienced before with my brother. This is one of those memories that I remember clearly: exactly where we were sitting in my backyard, and how he had looked so sad and troubled. Yet I had no idea of the depth of pain that he must have been experiencing. I have replayed that conversation in my mind so many times, trying to figure out how I could have asked him the right questions, to learn about how he was really feeling.

When trying to understand the experience of suicide, I think that Jack Jordan and Bob Baugher describe it well. 'Suicide is kind of like the perfect storm – it's the coming together of multiple factors in just the wrong way. This includes the person's biology, thinking, life circumstances, past life events, current stressors – all in just the wrong way that allows it to happen.'[23]

In my brother's case, the perfect storm was created by a number of factors, some that we know about and others that we will never know. One factor was the breakdown of his marriage to Tania, occurring sixteen months prior to Danny's suicide. I was very sad for both of them, especially as I had enjoyed a good relationship with my sister-in-law. They ended up selling their home and Danny moved into a granny flat in our local area. Danny had a tough time after that, but I rarely saw him look sad. There was only one time, when I looked at him in an unguarded moment, and he appeared despondent. But it was there and then gone. Blink, and you would have missed it. Danny was always joking around, so we never really knew what was happening for him emotionally.

He'd had other difficult life events over the past few years. He'd tried to form a new relationship, and it didn't work out. He then had a severe case of chickenpox, which is very painful when contracted as an adult. He was covered in them and, due to his contagiousness, our family wasn't able to visit him. He had a minor car accident.

Each of these factors – the breakdown of his marriage, the painful and prolonged case of adult chickenpox, a minor car accident, a failed attempt at forming a new relationship – were warning signs of the storm that was building, warning signs that we missed.

We did find out a few details we hadn't known. Danny had reached out to a work colleague and told her how he was feeling, that he was thinking about suicide. She had cared but had no idea how to help. We also learnt that he had been considering suicide for at least six months before he died. When we cleared out his accommodation, we found multiple suicide notes hidden under his mattress. We also found his divorce papers. They had arrived the day that he died, and lay there, open, at the front door. This was our sum of known factors.

I pleaded with his wife Tania to tell me what had gone wrong between them. I asked if she knew more about why Danny chose to die, but she wouldn't tell me. Her reasoning was that if Danny had chosen not to tell us the whole story, then it wasn't her role to do so. Maybe Danny had implored her not to talk about what had led to their marriage breakdown. Maybe Danny held secrets that he didn't want his family to know. I had no choice but to respect her decision, though I found it really hard. I wanted answers to my many unanswered questions, to the store of unknowns.

I never felt angry, as I know some do, when I was bereaved by suicide. Not at Danny. I just felt incredibly sad, and disappointed that Danny hadn't been able to move through what I now understand was unbearable pain. What we *do* know about suicide is that it is caused by what some have called psychache – a feeling of intense pain, anguish and aching, and a sense of hopelessness in the psyche – and there is no hope that the unbearable pain will ever ease. As John H. Hewett, author of *After Suicide*, says, it is a case of 'choosing to end unbearable pain, rather than choosing death'.[24]

Danny died when he was twenty-seven. He had his whole life ahead of him. He could have found love again, remarried, and been the wonderful husband, father, brother, son and uncle that he was meant to be. For these reasons, I am convinced of the importance of speaking out about how you are feeling. If you're feeling depressed and thinking that suicide is the only option, please seek help. If you can make it through that period of unbearable pain and speak to someone who cares – better still, someone who has the professional skills to listen and respond to your struggles – then you can emerge safely on the other side.

If this is you, feeling as though suicide is the only option, and you are convinced that there is *no* other option, so you don't want to speak to anyone about it, I want to tell you that talking to someone who knows what it is like to feel this way will impact your life. I know from lived experience, and from hearing the stories of others who have either been suicidal or have taken suicidal action, that life does and can change. I am a case in point: I thought that my life was doomed to always be the same, and that my pain would never cease. But it can and it does. Talking to someone who cares, who wants to hear your story, your perspective on why your life is so difficult, will help you to see other options.

There are so many resources available now for those who are grappling with suicidal depression. There are amazing telephone counselling services, such as Lifeline, Kids Helpline, Beyond Blue and MensLine Australia, as well as multiple sources of help through the internet. I also believe that everyone should have awareness of a few basic skills that can help save a life. Mental health first aid is as important as medical first aid. We can all learn how to help in a crisis situation.*

---

* See Appendix B: Mental Health First Aid Skills and Resources.

CHAPTER 12

LIFE AFTER THE LOSS OF MY BROTHER

Sometime in the aftermath of those shocking early days, I remembered something that had happened the night before I learnt of Danny's death. I had been watching a movie, fairly late at night. The rest of the family had all gone to bed. This movie was different to the usual kind that I would watch. It was sort of risqué, the type of movie that I wouldn't want anyone know I was watching. At some point, I suddenly felt a presence in the room with me. When I say presence, it was as though someone or something was there in the air around me. I looked around. Nothing. Then I paused the movie and walked around the house. There was no one there, everyone seemed to be deeply asleep. I went outside, and there were no cars or people around. At the time, I shrugged it off as my guilty conscience causing me to feel this way, and I went back to the movie. But I had felt a genuine sense of someone – not a threatening or scary presence – being in the lounge room with me. Thinking about it later, I understood it to be Danny's spirit coming to see me to say goodbye. While this may sound crazy or the product of an overactive imagination, there is a lot of evidence in the literature on grief and near-death experiences that would corroborate my experience that evening.

'They' (whoever they are) always say that you know who your friends are when you go through a tragedy. Well, I certainly discovered that my family and I were fortunate to have many supportive friends, family members, work colleagues, church family and others to support us, and to support my parents, in particular, who were carrying an immense burden. There were endless flowers, cards, phone calls, meals – all acknowledgements that Danny would be missed and our family was loved and cared for.

I spoke at my brother's funeral. I couldn't not do this. I had to honour the memory of my beautiful brother. I was the spokesperson for our family, sharing how much we loved Danny and presenting a biography of his too-short life. I spoke about what we had gained from living our lives alongside him and that we were trying to contemplate how we could live without him. We made the decision to bring Simone and Daniel to the funeral, to confront the fact of their uncle's passing, but left little Laura behind in the care of friends.

I remember feeling worried on the way to the funeral, concerned that I was feeling too composed, too together. Why was I not a complete and utter mess? Maybe I wouldn't cry at all? What would people think about that? Was there something wrong with me? As I walked, hand-in-hand with my family, to our church, I saw my brother John standing out the front, waiting for us. I began to howl. The sight of my brother, whom I loved – the only one I had now – completely undid me. The sobs and cries of my father during the service were unbearable, but, somehow, I managed to hold it together so that I could speak about Danny. After the service, I couldn't stop crying. As each person came up to me and expressed their sympathy, I cried anew. And I had worried that I wouldn't be able to cry!

The first year after losing Danny was very tough, as it is for each of us when we lose someone we love. The closer the relationship with the person, the longer and more intense the grieving process will be. It is a year of firsts. The first Christmas, New Year, birthday ... without Danny. It is unknown territory. Somehow, I fumbled my way through it. Mum and Dad were heartbroken, confronted by the unanswerable questions and the guilt that is such a common response to loss, especially by suicide.

One thing I learnt from my grief at this time was the importance of allowing time to mourn. If I felt the need to do something – no matter how odd it seemed or whatever time it was – I did it. I remember, during the first couple of weeks, I felt a strong compulsion to head to the beach, walk along the tideline and have some quiet time. I reflected on Danny, on my loss, and allowed space for my grief. Whenever I listened to that inner wisdom, I felt much better. But sometimes I thought these urges were foolish, which had to do with the strong sense of stoicism that my parents had instilled in me. It was always about being strong, and keeping on keeping on. I often felt as though my own insights were foolish or fanciful. I now know that nurturing ourselves through our pain and listening to our inner voice is an important part of self-care, which assists with the grieving process.

Facing the reality of death is the very hardest part of life. I remember seeing Danny everywhere – on the street when I was driving my car, in another car, and surely that was the shape of my brother's head, ahead in the shopping centre. Wasn't that him? I had to continually remind myself that Danny had died. I had to picture Danny in his coffin – we viewed his body before the church service. Having never seen a dead person before this time (let alone my beloved brother), I was fearful of what I would see. But I am glad that I did it. It was a chance to say goodbye. Also, the reality of seeing his body – with the spirit of Danny gone – proved to me that Danny really had died. Recalling that scene of Danny in the casket reminded me that I would never see Danny again, at least not in this life.

Additional to the loss of Danny was the loss of my sister-in-law Tania. During their marriage I had developed a close relationship with her, and I saw her as a friend as well as a family member. When Danny died, I rang Tania to talk things over. I had a twofold purpose in calling. I wanted her to come to the funeral service; I think I pleaded with her to come. I felt it was important that she be there for Danny, that he somehow needed her there. In my mind, I was convinced that Danny's spirit would be present at the funeral service. But Tania said that she couldn't attend because she had a young baby, who was only a few weeks old. She also said that it would be too difficult emotionally for her to come. I could certainly understand this. I knew it would take enormous strength and courage to go to the service, but I was unable not to feel disappointed about it. I saw Tania as part of our family, and so to me, at that time, it didn't feel right for her not to be part of his funeral service.

We have never seen Tania again. We tried many times to contact her but to no avail. It was another loss – the loss of my dear sister-in-law, the sister I'd never had. This led to many years of me looking out for Tania. If I was out and about, at our local Westfield shopping centre, or wherever, I would often see someone who looked like Tania. My hopes would rise, my heart would start to race, but when I got closer, I saw that it wasn't her. Another disappointment. It felt so important to connect with her because she was our connection to Danny. Ten years after Danny's death, at the request of my parents, I wrote to Tania (care of her brother, who lived locally) and asked if she would reconsider meeting with our family to talk about Danny. My mother had set her heart on Tania responding positively to this request. But the letter was never answered, nor responded to in any way. We don't even know if she received it. This made me feel very sad, as if an important connection to Danny had been lost.

During that difficult first year, a couple of strange things started happening in our family. I would find photos with Danny in them turned down. I would pop them up again, yet the next time I looked, they would again be turned face down. The culprit behind the photo turning, I discovered, was Daniel, aged seven. He said that it hurt too much to see the photos. So, they stayed down. Next, I started finding huge pieces of knotted hair hidden around the house, in corners of the lounge, under the lounge, in the bins. This was scary. I started to realise that Simone, aged ten at the time, was fiddling with her hair and accidently tying knots in it. Then, when she couldn't undo the knot, she would pull her hair out! I know, awful.

It reached the point that every time I would find a knotty piece of hair, my gut would quake with fear and dismay. Seeking to understand what was happening, I took Simone to a child psychologist, and she diagnosed her with trichotillomania,[25] also known as hair-pulling disorder. It is a form of obsessive-compulsive disorder that is triggered by anxiety. This was very sobering to learn. In retrospect, I think it was caused by a number of factors. Simone struggled with anxiety (both at this time and throughout her life), but at the time I think she was also responding to the stress in our household. We saw the psychologist a few times to help Simone work through her feelings of anxiety and the grief she was experiencing at the loss of her beloved uncle. Eventually, she stopped pulling her hair out. She just continued to fiddle with her hair, constantly.

The psychologist also diagnosed Simone with Asperger's – or high-functioning autism – what is now referred to as autism spectrum disorder. This was even harder to accept. It was something that I had never even contemplated. She based her diagnosis on the social issues that Simone struggled with, her past history, her difficulty with making eye contact (present since she was a baby) and her obsessions with various hobbies, such as Harry Potter, computer games, reading, art and craft. It is also a comorbid condition that often overlaps with ADHD.

I was initially unable to accept this diagnosis. I could accept the ADHD but, at the time, I perceived autism as a frightening and permanent condition. Now, with the benefit of further reading and reflection, I have accepted that Simone possibly did suffer from this mild form of autism. I have also wondered if perhaps my mother had Asperger's. The clues were there. Mum and Simone were very similar in character. My mum struggled with emotions – both with experiencing them and expressing them. Perhaps what I had always put down as Mum's Dutch stoicism was actually Asperger's. It would explain why Mum had such a hard time coping with my emotional reactivity *and* why she struggled to demonstrate her love in a way that was perceived as love by me.

When my brother died, I was already struggling. My old nemesis, postnatal depression, came back to haunt me. I remember Mum coming to visit me one day. I tried to make an effort to be engaging and welcoming, but it obviously wasn't working. On her departure Mum commented, 'You know, it's not nice coming to visit you when you can't smile and you look so unhappy.' Those words hurt and angered me deeply. My mother had no idea, back then, about what I was going through. She looked to me to give her comfort and support during her own grief experience, and I do understand that. As a parent who has experienced the loss of a child, I know that she must have been talking from the perspective of her own grief. However, I was also struggling, with a double-barrelled problem, depression and grief.

In addition, I was experiencing a crisis in my faith for the first time, and I felt defenceless and hopeless. I had gone back to my university studies just before I fell pregnant with Laura and I was experiencing doubts about the veracity of my faith. I'd always had a simple, childlike faith in God, which had stood me in good stead. I had been going to church since the day I was born and I'd never had reason to doubt. But, with the new wisdom and understanding that comes with a university education, I had started to question everything.

Part of this questioning was worrying about where Danny was now. My understanding of suicide, at the time, was that suicide was an unforgivable sin, and that Danny may not have made it to heaven due to the choice he'd made to end his own life. Our pastor, however, was completely reassuring about Danny's choice to suicide. His perspective was that Danny was now at home with God, the Father. Danny had come home early, but he was still home. He also stated that there was no biblical reference to suicide being an unforgivable sin. I really wanted to believe and hang on to those words, but my fears and doubts continued. I took to reading any books I could find about what happens after death, from people who had near-death experiences. There is a whole realm of literature, both Christian and otherwise, to consult. Some of this reading was comforting and some of it was scary. I considered seeing a medium, but I had a fear of consulting anything that was not Christian in origin.

What helped me the most was the vision of a Christian friend of mine. This was a woman who knew how to pray, and who had been through enormous health challenges. She was a woman with a deep personal faith, who had experienced authentic visions from God. She told me that she had a vision of Danny in heaven playing with children. She said that his face was glowing with peace and contentment, and that the message he had for me and the family was, 'Don't worry about me, I am at peace.' I held on to this vision whenever insidious doubts and fears arose.

I have been able to draw from my own experiences of grief, through the loss of my brother to suicide, in many ways over the years. Initially, I was a volunteer facilitator of a suicide support group. Later, I made use of it in my work for Lifeline, the crisis telephone counselling service. Later still, I coordinated and co-facilitated a suicide support group. I have also spoken at various services and events, in the hope that my personal story might assist others who are bereaved by suicide. The process of drawing on my own suffering to help others heal their hearts has also helped in the healing of my wounds.

CHAPTER 13

LOSING MUM

Christmas fell on a Monday that year, in 2006, but we decided to go to church on the Sunday as well. At 10.00 am, we were sitting in church, when I felt a strong compulsion to visit Mum after the service. I leaned over to Tony and said, 'I know that we're going to see Mum for Christmas tomorrow, but I have this really strong feeling that I need to visit Mum today.' He agreed. I am so glad that I listened to my gut feeling that day. Things had been awkward between Mum and me. She had mentioned, yet again, that I wasn't giving her enough time and attention, and I was feeling the habitual pangs of guilt. It felt important to give her some additional care before Christmas Day.

I remember that Mum was sitting on the coffee table, and she kept wiping her glasses clean, over and over again. I noticed that she seemed a little more forgetful and vaguer than usual. I was especially aware of changes in Mum because a few months earlier she had been diagnosed with Alzheimer's disease. Mum had sought a diagnosis because three of her sisters had already been diagnosed and were suffering different stages of the illness. It was a brave decision for her to make, I thought. Early diagnosis was good because it meant that she could start on medication that would delay its progression. Yet it also felt heartbreaking for Mum to be given another health condition to endure. And this had to be one of the worst. I knew that Mum was very anxious about how the illness would advance. We all were. It felt so unfair!

The next day – Christmas morning – the kids invaded our bedroom, wanting to open their Santa sacks, happy and excited. The phone rang at 7.30 am. It was my dad. 'I think Will has had a stroke.' (Or some version of this because he was speaking in Dutch). 'The ambulance is on the way. Come to the hospital as soon as you can.' In the background, I could hear my mum calling out, also in Dutch.

My first reaction, which lasted for a heartbeat, was anger. Then dismay. *Really? Today?* My second response – an erroneous one, as it turned out – was that this would be a minor stroke. This was partly because I had heard Mum's voice, loud and clear, during the phone call. My knowledge of strokes was also limited; everyone I knew who had parents who had suffered a stroke had suffered a minor one. So, I made the decision that we would go to church first and then go to the hospital.

Good one, Connie!

Sitting in church, my heart thudded heavily and my stomach lurched. *What are we doing here?* I thought. *We have to go to the hospital. Now.* We dropped Laura and Matthew at their other grandparents' house with a quick explanation, and took Simone and Daniel with us to the local hospital. Mum was in casualty, and the minister of their church was in attendance.

We were all in this small cubicle – Mum, Dad, my brother John, Tony, Simone, Daniel, the minister and me. Why was the minister here? I quickly found out. He took me aside, out of the cubicle. He told me that Mum had experienced a major bleed in her brain, and that it was really important that I take time now to talk to Mum while she could still listen and respond. He obviously knew a lot more about strokes than I did. I felt fuzzy and confused. What? Now? Talk now?

I looked at Mum. She was staring at me intently. I looked at Tony, and at Simone and Daniel, who looked equally shocked and confused. Then I spoke to Mum. I told her how much I loved her. And how much I admired her strength and tenacity in the face of all the health challenges she had experienced. I told her how strong she was coming to Australia by herself, knowing only Dad, and starting a new life for herself.

I think I garbled. I couldn't fully grasp the enormity of what was happening. Mum couldn't speak back, but she smiled deeply at me. She tried to raise her arm, but her arm wasn't responding. She was trying to point to her head, which must have been hurting her. Simone and Daniel both spoke with her and hugged her. They were crying. I don't remember crying and I can't remember if I hugged her. Soon after that, Mum closed her eyes and lost consciousness.

The doctor took us to that small room where you receive bad news. He explained that Mum's stroke was serious. They had done scans and discovered that she had experienced a major brain haemorrhage. He explained that they could operate, but even if the operation was successful, her quality of life would be limited. She would be bedridden and would not recover the use of the left side of her body. He asked us to make a decision on how to proceed. As soon as possible.

I had no bloody idea! I didn't want to make this decision. I couldn't. Thankfully, Dad could. He said that he had spoken to Mum about what she wanted in the case of a stroke, because Mum's mother had also had a stroke. She'd had a severe stroke, and the family had decided to proceed with the operation, against her wishes. She had lingered on for another eighteen months, in a nursing home, with limited quality of life. Mum had said to Dad that if she ever had a stroke, he was not to keep her alive. He had to let her go. I remember feeling relieved that I didn't have to make this momentous decision, because I didn't have it in me to decide. I loved my mum. I also felt as though she had suffered enough, but I couldn't decide to let her die. That was too big for me.

Soon afterwards, the hospital transported Mum to the Prince of Wales Hospital, as they had the required intensive care equipment. We were advised to go home, and to return in a few hours. I remember walking into the thick, hot, yellow sunshine, feeling shocked and numb. How could this be happening today, of all days? How could people be going on with Christmas Day when my mother was dying?

We were all very quiet. We decided to go to my sister-in-law's place, where Christmas lunch was being held. It was a strange meal. Tony's mother kept saying that it would be all right, that Mum would pull through. Simone decided that she would like to come back to the hospital with us, to stay with Mum and say goodbye. She was nineteen at the time. By this stage, I was feeling extremely ill. I had a migraine and felt extremely nauseous. Grief can be a very physical experience.

We didn't talk much. We arrived at the hospital and walked through the hospital grounds, feeling a strong sense of unreality. How could this be happening on Christmas Day? Did anyone know or care about what was happening to us? I remember looking at people's faces; everything appeared so ordinary. But I felt surreal. Everything was in extra-sharp detail, and looking at it hurt my eyes. Everything hurt.

We sat by the hospital bed. It was my childhood, revisited. Mum was lying in a strange hospital ward with all this equipment hooked up to her. The same smells were there – sterility and cleanliness; the same feeling was in the air. I held Mum's hand and talked to her, which was what the intensive care nurse suggested. So did Simone. She was so strong. Dad was there, too, of course, sitting on the other side of the bed and quietly holding Mum's hand. Tony was there as well, hovering in the background.

After a few hours, the nurse suggested that we go home. She explained that Mum could linger on for days. It was a matter of when her body started to let go. She explained that we could be there all night, and then leave to go the bathroom and Mum could go in just those few short minutes. We went home. I drove. I felt too sick to be a passenger. I needed to do something.

The kids and I sat on the lounge and hugged each other. Matthew was too young to really understand what was happening. He was seven, Laura was eleven, Daniel was sixteen, and Simone, as mentioned, was nineteen. The next day, Boxing Day, we spent at the hospital. I still had a migraine and felt really unwell. I felt as though I needed to lie down and rest, but I also didn't want to leave my mum. I said to Mum, 'If you want me to stay, squeeze my hand.' She squeezed my hand. Hard.

We stayed. I talked to Mum. I stared at her arm and noticed her dry skin and age spots. I hugged her arm. For months afterwards, the vision of her arm remained in my mind, appearing at odd moments. The nurse said that I could lie down next to her and hug her if I wanted to. I did want to, but it felt too strange. Lying next to her felt as though it might be an invasion of her peace and space. It was weird to be sitting there, talking, and not knowing whether she could hear or understand, but the nurses told us that hearing is the last sense to leave us when we are dying, so I persisted.

Simone drew a sketch of Mum. It was heartbreaking. I felt really unwell and as if I, too, was dying, but on the inside. The hospital encouraged us to leave, at about 3.00 pm. When we reached home,

I went straight to bed. My head was whirling, but I have no idea what I was thinking about. An hour later, the hospital rang. They advised us to return to the hospital as soon as we could, as the end was near. It was an hour's drive away. Once again, I had to drive. I needed to do something; it was too hard to just sit.

We arrived too late. All of us did, including Dad.

A lovely nurse told us that she had stayed with Mum and held her hand, so that she wasn't alone in that last hour of life.

I felt terrible that we had left the hospital, that we left Mum to die without her family around her. I was angry at Dad that he hadn't stayed. I was angrier at myself for my weakness. I thought what a selfish family we were to desert Mum in this way. We all said our final goodbyes, including Simone. Tony drove us home. Simone and I sat on the lounge, with our arms wrapped around each other. We were very quiet, just sharing a few words and tears together. Simone was very, very special to my mum. They had always shared a special bond.

What happened next was inexplicable, and it's difficult to describe. I looked to my right, and, suddenly, there was Mum. But she was not the mother I ever remember seeing. I can only describe it as there being a circular hole in the space next to me, and Mum was within it. It was like a cameo. She looked beautiful; she was young, maybe in her early twenties or thirties, but I don't ever remember seeing her like this, nor even seeing a photo where she looked like this, and I haven't seen one since. She wore a white dress, with a red rose pinned to it, close to her face. Mum's expression was radiant. She appeared joyful and full of peace and contentment.

She spoke to me, but not in an audible way. I just felt her words. She said to me, 'Love Simone, love Simone, love Simone.' Then she was gone.

'Please don't go,' I said out loud.

'What?' asked Simone.

'Mum, she was just there. She told me to love you.'

Simone hadn't seen or experienced it, only me. What a beautiful gift she had given me. The reassurance that life goes on after death.

I was not surprised by her words. They were exactly what I would have expected my mother to say. She knew about the struggles I had in my relationship with Simone, and she loved Simone deeply. It made total sense that these would be her final words to me. Nearly two years later, her words came back to haunt me, after we lost Simone. My mum knew … She knew that Simone was going to die, and she needed to tell me to value my time with her, to love her. It was a warning. If only I had been able to register her message on a deeper level. It all seemed so clear, now that it was too late.

All my life, I had worried about losing Mum. As she had chronic health problems, it had been a real possibility, one that could happen at any time. As a child, I remember thinking, *I cannot live if something happens to my mum.* I depended on her so much. Naturally, all children need their mothers, and maybe my need for her was as strong as any other child, but I remember feeling as though I couldn't live life without her.

As I entered my adolescent years, I slowly became more independent, but my emotional need for my mother continued to be intense. Mum was my strength, my life's blood. She was safety, security and love personified. If anything happened in my life, I wanted to talk to my mum about it, to ask her opinion. After marriage, much of my need for security and safety was transferred to Tony. But my connection with my mother remained strong. Now it had happened, my greatest childhood fear. And, just as I did after losing Danny, I felt numb.

First shock. Then numbness. Then nothing, a great empty hole of nothing. No wailing, screaming, crying hysterically or shouting, as I had anticipated might happen. Numbness is the body's way of protecting us, but that dull sense of nothingness didn't feel right. What was wrong with me?

Once again, this time at Mum's funeral, I spoke as the representative of our immediate family. I spoke about Mum's life in Holland with her big and loving family, and the life she built in Australia, with her family and the relationships she developed with many people. I spoke about her strength in the face of chronic illness. Mum would often say to me, 'Connie, there is always someone worse off than you,' and, 'Think of the other person first, what it must feel like for them.' These were maxims that she lived by.

She never felt sorry for herself. Even though her life was tough, she rarely complained. While I might have known how she was feeling, others would rarely know how much she suffered. She always put on such a bright and positive face. I spoke of Mum's great love and care for our family, and how she set a great example for us – in our faith, and in caring for others in a loving and practical way. Mum was always sewing, knitting or making crafts, for people in need or for church charities and missions.

Mum always donated to charities, even though our financial situation was not strong, and her sense of social justice was inspiring. She accepted everyone equally and never put on airs or graces. I remember her befriending and caring for those with mental illness. As a child, they scared me because they looked and acted so unusually, but Mum stressed the importance of caring for everyone, no matter what.

She also had compassion for the disenfranchised, especially Australia's First Nations peoples and African Americans. She was a big reader, and she inspired me to develop a love of books and reading. The dominant aspect of Mum, however, was her quality of being down-to-earth, full of common sense and practical wisdom. This was the greatest gift she left me, a wistful young woman who needed a dose of pragmatism in her life.

After the funeral, it was Dad and Simone who seemed to take Mum's death the hardest. Simone had been very close to her Oma (the Dutch term for grandma) and was deeply affected by her loss. In her preschool days, Mum was a regular carer for Simone when I was working part-time. She often took her to the local park and they would feed the ducks, as well as sharing many special one-on-one activities. This continued as Simone grew up. My mum seemed to have a genuine empathy for and understanding of Simone, which strengthened the bond between them.

In her early days of grief, Simone struggled, as she felt as though her friends and church family didn't understand or empathise enough. It seemed as if no one else in her circle had experienced the loss of a grandparent or a close relative, and she found this really isolating.

She painted an artwork, *The Greatest Emotions are Indescribable*, that illustrated how she was feeling. In her artist's statement she wrote:

> This body of work was created in response to my own grief over the loss of my Oma, following the stroke she had on Christmas Day, and shortly after her death on Boxing Day. As we sat crying on Christmas Day, the idea of opening presents was an anathema. We came to find that words simply couldn't describe how we were feeling. Similarly, a descriptive image of the scenes that unfolded in the hospital, or in our daily lives following the tragedy, couldn't explain the emotions I felt inside.

Throughout my grief experience, everyday belongings that Oma possessed, and daily events reminiscent of the days spent together, became a ghostly reminder of her, and a cause for great sadness. I became much more aware of my emotions through the experience, which suddenly helped me to feel the urge and ease of expressing myself on paper abstractly, rather than realistically, which used to be my natural tendency.

With ink, acrylic, pastels, crayon, fluorescent pens and biros and whatever I could grab hold of that instantaneously appealed to me, I threw down colours, shapes, lines, patterns, marks that naturally arose in me, to describe what I was feeling.

Within these paper responses to my own grief, I found myself subconsciously using subjects reminiscent of Oma's Dutch history through tulips, the colour blue (with Delft blue pottery) and windmills. Pale skin colours and pale yellows, swirls of confusion, half-forgotten early childhood memories of times I spent in the Camellia Gardens at Caringbah with her, sunset representing my own grief shining over me but never reaching the end of the horizon and its conclusion, while images and colours and textures of the bush and seas contorted in the images which I draw pleasure from.

Interlocking hands with contrasting colours meeting each other as holding Oma's hand in hospital and her saddened eyes looking at me – the last time she opened her eyes. Or are they the eyes of my Opa? Mum? Dad? Brothers? Sister? Myself?

I think these observations form a beautiful expression of Simone's artistic vision and the deep love and connection that she felt with her Oma. It was a treasure for me to find these expressions of Simone's feelings of grief because they reveal so much about the way she saw the world and her relationships. It's strange to think that Simone wrote these words about grief and loss, not knowing that less than two years later, we would be experiencing similar grief about losing her.

During the first few months after losing Mum, I focused on supporting my kids in their grief, and also my dad. I put my own grief on the back shelf and focused my attention where I thought it was most needed. I wasn't conscious of doing this at the time but, looking back, that's what I did.

Dad had a very different way of grieving than me; this is normal, of course, as we each have our own way of coping with loss. I like to hold on to everything that belonged to my loved one – I want to wear it, smell it, breathe it in, feel it, and keep it forever. My dad wanted to remove all vestiges of Mum's life as soon as possible. Within a week of the funeral, he had thrown out all Mum's medicines from the fridge and cupboard. Within two weeks, he had gone through Mum's clothes and belongings, sorting them and wanting me to decide what I wanted to keep for myself and my girls, and what he could give to charity. I asked him not to rush, observing that he might be sorry later that he had removed everything, but his response was prosaic. 'Why keep all of this stuff? I don't need it. She doesn't need it anymore.' He seemed to think I was foolish in wanting to hang on to Mum's belongings when they were no longer useful.

I found this process really painful. I wasn't ready to get rid of anything. But Dad's attitude was out of sight, out of mind; he didn't want any reminders of Mum. I guess that while Mum's things brought me comfort, they brought him pain. Bit by bit, Dad removed everything to do with Mum. All he kept was one photo. He gave me all the photos of our family life – of Mum, of my children with Mum, all of it.

After that, Dad swung between being almost too together, as though he was relieved that Mum had gone, and becoming very needy. I wondered if the burden of caring for Mum over their lifetime had been too heavy for him; while he grieved her loss, it also freed him. Mum's chronic ill health must have been very difficult and stressful. Yet at other times, Dad would ring me multiple times a day, which was very out of character. He suffered from mood swings, and his physical ailments increased. Dad already had problems with his back and neck, and these increased during the first months after we lost Mum.

One weekend, about three months after Mum died, I went to a Lifeline retreat for staff and volunteers, in the Blue Mountains. It was a special time of connecting with ourselves and one another. One of the activities we did was meditation, with a yoga practitioner. It started out innocently enough, with breathing and chanting. I hadn't done much meditation before. *Ah, this is nice, it's so relaxing*, I thought. Then, suddenly, I was in a world of pain. Out of nowhere, tears started to rain down and I began to sob. All I could see was Mum – at Sutherland Hospital in casualty, at Prince of Wales Hospital, where I was holding her hand and hugging her arm. The feeling of pain was deeply physical, I was a thudding bag of sadness, grief and loss. *Was this normal?* I wondered. Does meditation bring out all the grief that you have buried?

It was a good place to feel the reality of my grief. I was surrounded by counsellors, in a nurturing and safe location. One lady, Anne, a lovely woman – warm, nurturing and caring – just held me and let me cry. I didn't need to tell her what was going on. She knew of my loss.

It was a healing time, but it didn't feel like it in the moment. Grief hurts. But there is no way to avoid it. Grief has to be felt, to be experienced. And it won't be just once. Whenever the pain of loss hits you, the only way through it is to feel it. That's where the healing process lies. I was an unwilling hostage to these awful feelings of pain, but I knew that experiencing these emotions was what I needed to do. I had read about the experience, I understood it intellectually, but now I had to feel it in my heart because that is where we heal.

How can you expect not to suffer from the loss of someone who means so much to you, who has loved and cared for you throughout your whole life? As the song says, and it's no cliché: 'Love hurts'. The more you love, the greater your pain. It's the cost of loving, but who would be without the gift of love?

It is really difficult to have the anniversary of losing Mum at Christmastime. Every Christmas is a sad reminder of Mum, at a time that is meant to be a joyous celebration of love and family. The first couple of Christmases were particularly painful. Early in the morning, I would remember the phone call from Dad telling us about Mum's stroke. I would dread any phone calls. Then, when we went to church, I would remember how I'd made the decision to go to church when I should have gone directly to the hospital. I tortured myself, wondering if Mum would still have been able to talk to me before she fell into the coma if we had arrived earlier. Sitting in church, I would have the same physical feelings I'd had on the day of her stroke. It was so difficult that I suggested to the family that instead of going back to the same church and the same service, that we either go to church on Christmas Eve or go to another church. They agreed and that did help somewhat.

The other issue is that Mum's birthday is on New Year's Eve. It felt as though the whole Christmas/New Year period was dominated by the sadness of losing Mum. I usually try to go to the cemetery where her ashes are interred either on Boxing Day or New Year's Eve, to bring flowers and have a chat. That does bring some comfort.

One of the hardest parts about losing Mum was not being able to call her and tell her any special news about what was happening in our family. Whenever something happened – one of the kids received a school award, or there was news about a friend, or when Simone had her hair cut in a new style – I was reminded that she would never know. Or when there was bigger news, such as when my brother John started dating for the first time in twenty years, or when my son Daniel started going out with the girlfriend who would become his wife, any one of myriad significant moments in life, I wanted to share them with Mum.

I knew that Mum would always have been interested and would have cared about what was happening in our lives. When Mum died, it felt as if I'd lost my whole family, because Mum and I would talk a few times a week, I would usually visit Mum once a week and Mum would visit us every week or fortnight. All of a sudden, that contact ended. Mum was the one who maintained the family connections. Dad was more comfortable at home, and he didn't have a need to be in contact or visit much. All of a sudden, my family felt very small; just my brother John, Dad and me. And I didn't often see or hear from them, as both were pretty introverted men, so I felt quite alone.

It wasn't the last time that grief caught me unawares. It's a continuing theme in my story.

CHAPTER 14

INSIGHTS ABOUT GRIEF

Underlying in each of my experiences of grief has been an intense sense of emotional numbness. What I was feeling didn't seem enough – not compared to what I considered an appropriate emotional response to loss, especially the loss of Simone. This numbness worried me intensely, and continued to worry me over the following years.

Due to my inherent emotional fragility, I expected that I would fall apart if something happened to one of my children. I would be reduced to a helpless mess; I would take to my bed and be totally unable to function. Because I was still functioning and it was so hard to cry, I thought I must be heartless. I thought there was something wrong with me, that I must not have loved Simone enough, that my grief was not normal.

It bothered me that I could cry so easily about the loss of Emma (a young fashion student whom I knew for a short time through Lifeline) and David, a dear Lifeline friend (whom I had known for about eighteen months), and, later, about my beautiful friend Diana (who tragically died of cancer after a difficult life), but not be able to find the same release and comfort through tears for Simone, my own daughter.

Emma had been a member of the small Lifeline training group that I was facilitating, and I was drawn to her warmth and charisma. She had that radiant inner light that I spoke of earlier (which Simone had) and which I am naturally drawn to. She amazed all who knew her as a truly beautiful soul, both inside and out. Six weeks into the course, Lifeline holds an intensive training weekend, to get to know the other trainees in the relaxed setting of the Royal National Park. Emma was part of that training and I was touched by the beauty of her spirit when I witnessed her responses.

Three days later, I learnt that Emma had died in a tragic pedestrian accident. I felt devastated. I could not understand how God could take an angel like Emma away from the world, when she had so much to offer. A group from Lifeline made the trip to the funeral in Orange to acknowledge the importance of Emma to the Lifeline community. I have never forgotten that funeral. There were well over a thousand people in attendance, standing room only. There were hymns sung that day that I have trouble singing to this day. As Emma was similar in age to Simone, it also struck close to home.

It was eighteen months later when we lost Simone. Later, during my grief, I wondered if it was another sign from the universe that I should have been paying attention to. It was certainly a stark reminder of the fragility of life and how we never know what tomorrow will hold.

I spoke of this discrepancy – between my ability to grieve for Emma but not Simone – in sessions with my psychologist. In one session, I realised I held an enormous amount of fear about confronting and feeling the full weight of losing Simone. My psychologist had asked me to choose a cushion to represent my feelings of grief for Simone.

I chose a large multicoloured cushion with a complex web of intersecting lines and patterns. When asked why I chose this particular one I answered that it was because my grief felt so complex and complicated. Every thought, feeling and behaviour was intricately interconnected. I felt so much guilt, shame and depression about our relationship that I was afraid it would swallow me whole.

I have learnt over time that there is no wrong way or right way to grieve. Every person has a unique way of responding to grief. Our sorrow is shaped by the relationship we have experienced with our loved one, and our own individual temperament. The closer the relationship, the harder the loss. The circumstances of the loss, whether it is sudden, unexpected, traumatic or anticipated, will also influence the kind of grief we experience.

What I have learnt about my experience of grief is that when I lose someone close to me, I push the pain, sadness and grief away. It is too intense and overwhelming. That is what happened when I lost Danny, and it was the same when I lost my mum.

Eventually, I became aware that I had been putting off grieving Simone for a long time, pretty much right from the start. But it took a long time to realise it. I was in denial, a state described by many writers, such as Elisabeth Kübler-Ross, as being the first of four stages of grief.[*] In my case, I was also in denial that I was in denial! It's amazing the many ways we can fool ourselves, in order to survive. And that's exactly what I was doing, that was the reason for my experience of emotional numbness. I know this now, and am able to understand

---

[*] Elisabeth Kübler-Ross and J. William Worden discuss the four (or five) stages of grief.

my reactions, though at the time I could only judge and condemn. My grief was complex because our relationship was complicated, and it wasn't straightforward to express.

One thing I have learnt about myself is that I 'don't do' sadness and grief. Depression and anxiety, yes, they have been constant companions. Anger – I have known that emotion far too well. But sadness – *avoid*! Grief – protect, defend, procrastinate. And this is coming from a counsellor who tells her clients that the only way to heal from grief is to feel it, to experience it. However, on some level I must have known that I was pushing away my grief about Simone. I recall telling friends and family that while I may look okay now, in a few years' time, when people would expect me to be in a better place emotionally, that would be the time when it would hit me. Then, I would fall apart.

But I continued to question and torture myself. My inner critic had plenty of ammunition to shoot me down, and give me that same familiar message: 'Not good enough, Connie. You can't even grieve properly!' I hated it when people would comment on how well I was coping with the death of Simone. I knew they meant well, and it was said in a spirit of encouragement. Then they would comment on how upset Tony was, or how hard it was on our family, how sad the kids were. But how great was it that I was coping well? It felt like an accusation. There was something wrong with me; I was cold-hearted. And I agreed with them. I should be devastated; I should be a complete mess. I also agreed that I did seem to be coping well. On the outside, I was. On the inside, I was a confused, complex whirl of emotions.

When my guilt and sadness overtook me, I would often talk to Tony about how confused I felt about my relationship with Simone. How guilty I continued to feel, how I wasn't even sure if Simone really loved me, because of how things were between us. He told me that he and Simone had talked about the struggles in my relationship with her. He said, 'Simone always knew that you loved her. She didn't like it when you got angry, but she never doubted your love.' It was reassuring at the time, but was hard for me to fully accept.

Other times I would call Erica, Simone's best friend. I asked her, 'Did Simone hate me? Did she tell you about how tough our relationship was?' It was too hard to ask the unbidden questions on my lips: 'Do you think she loved me, cared about me? Did she know how much I loved her?'

Erica never failed to reassure me. She told me that Simone often spoke about me and the family. She said, 'Simone knew that you loved her, without a shadow of a doubt.' She reassured me that Simone didn't hold any grievances against me. I wanted to believe her. I would hold on to that, until the next set of fears and doubts began.

Much later, I realised that I didn't feel as though I deserved to grieve Simone, because I hadn't been a good enough mother. Only good mothers were allowed to grieve the loss of their children. I was not a good mother, so I had no entitlement to grieve. This was a huge realisation, which marked a new level of awareness. This realisation was deepened through some training I attended about family relationships. One of the video tapes that was shown was far too close to home. It was about a mother who was struggling in her relationship with her eldest daughter. As I watched the video and witnessed the struggles between them, I had one of those light-bulb moments. The reason I was so hard on Simone was because I loved her so much. If I hadn't loved her so much, I wouldn't have tried so hard. If I hadn't cared, I wouldn't have become so angry and frustrated. That was why the mother on the video was angry: she cared so much. I became so emotional and uncomfortable that I had to leave.

I walked to the nearby beach and sat in the sand, feeling very sad. The beach was deserted, so I sat alone and cried. This knowledge had come far too late. Why didn't I comprehend this while Simone was with us? How could I fix it now? While I sat there, sort of hoping that one of my colleagues would come out and check on me, I had a vision. I had started thinking about how sad I was that Simone would not be involved with her friend Erica's wedding. She had recently become engaged, and I was sure that Simone would have been her bridesmaid if she hadn't died. I felt so sad about the many losses to come: the weddings she wouldn't be part of, the many experiences of life that Simone would never enjoy. My sadness deepened.

As I sat there, I had a vision of Simone, walking towards me along the beach. She was wearing a beautiful, long, silky, cream dress, as I had anticipated her wearing as Erica's bridesmaid. I walked up to meet her. She held out her hands and spoke to me, but not in audible words. The sense I had from her was that she loved me and forgave me. It was a beautiful experience. It only lasted a few minutes but, afterwards, I walked away feeling more peaceful and whole than I had for a very long time.

As time passed, I struggled with giving myself permission to feel my grief. I always seemed to feel sad at the wrong time. I was waiting for the perfect time when I had no other distractions or responsibilities to attend to. I may have been driving to work, for instance, so I would think, *I can't cry now, I need to focus on the road and prepare myself for clients.* Or I would be at work and a session would stir up my grief, and, of course, that was not a good time. Or I would be out with friends, at the movies or shopping. After a while, I realised that there was never going to be a perfect time to grieve. I had three children, a husband and a job; there was always going to be some other priority. I realised that, sometimes, you need to stop, put all else aside and grieve. As Karen Katafiasz observes in *Grief Therapy*,[26] while we may try to divert our attention away from pain or push it down, at some point our feelings of grief will make themselves heard.

One of the best pieces of advice I received about grief was from a friend and fellow counsellor who experienced the traumatic loss of two of her children. She used the analogy of a mother nurturing her baby as a parallel for our need to nurture and care for our grief. If we don't pay attention to our grief, it will cry and act out in the same way that a baby will if we don't love and care for them. This may mean, she explained, taking time for ourselves if we are suddenly impacted by grief. She told me that one day she was at the wedding of one of her friend's daughters, when she was suddenly caught out by grief. She explained that, consequently, she spent most of the wedding reception in the ladies' room crying her heart out because she would never experience the marriage of her youngest daughter.

I found this analogy particularly helpful and relevant. I am someone who tends to put other matters and other people before myself. I would consider it selfish to focus on my own sadness, or I would worry about how others might perceive me if I was to put my own feelings first. But I learnt over time – the hard way – that sometimes the most important thing I can do is to honour and respect my own grief when I am feeling it. Over time, I have become better at allowing myself the time and space to grieve.

And, over time, I was finally able to genuinely feel and express my grief. Sometimes with my therapist, sometimes on my own. Sometimes a passage in a book about grief, or a movie, or a memory, would resonate and I would lose myself in sadness. Huge, painful sobs would wash over me, like dumpers at the beach, tossing my emotions about and spitting me out the other side. It was so painful. Words are inadequate to explain how much it hurt. But, afterwards, there would be a sense of calmness and peace. I would feel some relief.

Of course, I was not the only one suffering. My family was also suffering and they needed me. Tony was totally gutted. He had never been one to cry, but he cried a lot, especially during that first year, which was the hardest year for him. When I was still in the depths of denial (and denial that I was in denial), Tony was having a tough time. I remember trying to reassure him, making, I realised later, glib statements and superficial reassurances that failed to address the depths of the despair and misery that he was feeling.

Tony also grieved in a different way to me. I needed to talk; Tony didn't want to talk. He pushed me away whenever I would ask him to share how he felt with me. He wanted to grieve on his own, and on his own terms. This is not an uncommon response by men – many tend to retreat, internalise and process their feelings in their own way and their own time.

Daniel was bereft. He had lost his best friend and his sister. They were extremely close. I was really worried about how he would survive this loss. However, Daniel, and Laura, too, were surrounded and encouraged by support from their friendship groups, youth group leaders and youth group, and wider church family, which did help them both.

In the early days, Laura seemed to be coping well, but I later learnt that she was trying to be strong for all of us (not an unusual experience for children going through family turmoil). Sadly, Laura's grief caught up with her a year or two later when she started to suffer severe anxiety and panic attacks in the classroom, accompanied by strong and confusing physical symptoms. I tried to help Laura to work through her grief, but I was too close to her and her struggles. She needed the help of a therapist outside the family, so she saw a psychologist for a while to help her process her grief and related feelings.

Matthew, after the initial shock, seemed to be coping fine – at the age of nine, he seemed to be resilient. As Simone was twelve years older than him, he didn't have as much of a relationship with her as Daniel and Laura did. Matthew had also lost an uncle he'd never had the chance to know and his grandmother. I wondered if he thought that early death was normal. He had experienced so much of it.

Simone's grandparents, aunts and uncles were devastated. Tony's parents still struggle to speak about Simone without tears in their eyes. My friends and Simone's friends were also suffering. When I was touched by the grief of my family, friends or others, I put my own grief aside and focused on helping them. This was not a conscious process; it was simply my automatic reaction.

As I write about my grief, I need to highlight how fundamental my Christian faith has been to the way I have grieved Simone. If I didn't believe in life after death, and that I will be reunited with Simone upon my death, this story would be very different. While I have had my share of doubts and questions over different aspects of the Bible, I have no doubt that Simone is with God, in heaven. If I didn't believe this, I don't know how I could have survived my grief. I would not be the same person who is writing this book.

On my bad days, this belief is all I have to hold on to. I don't know how those who have lost loved ones survive without this inner faith. Knowing that I will see and be with her again, along with Mum,

Danny and other loved ones, has sustained me on the tough days. It has also kept me grounded in my faith, and has been supported not only by the gospels from the New Testament, but also in accounts written by those who have had near-death experiences or experiences with dying people. These books have been written by both Christians and those with no previous religious faith.

CHAPTER 15

ONGOING STRUGGLES WITH GRIEF

One of the continuing challenges I faced was the dilemma of how to answer the seemingly innocuous question about how many children I have. When you meet someone new you tend to talk about general topics, including your family. For a long time, I would start becoming anxious when the topic turned to family because I knew that sooner or later *that* question would be asked. My heart would race and I would feel a cold, dull sense of dread, as I reflected on how I would respond.

In the early months and years, I would find a way to avoid giving a direct answer. I might start by giving names and ages, and with Simone I would say how old she would have been in the year that I was being asked. After a while, that started to feel weird, as I have always strived to be honest. So, I tried saying that I have three children. But this was awful. It was even more of a lie. I have four children; Simone is just no longer with us.

I have finally come up with a way of responding that works for me. If I am meeting someone with whom I will have a continuing relationship, such as a work colleague or a new friend, I will tell them the truth, if and when they ask. I never bring it up otherwise. I say that

I have four children – two girls, two boys, their ages – and provide a short explanation that my eldest daughter died in a car accident when she was twenty-one. I have found it easier just to be upfront. I want to get the brutal reality out of the way, so that I won't carry the anxiety that I will have to tell them one day. It's never an easy conversation, but over time I have grown accustomed to it. If I'm meeting someone casually, in a one-off encounter where I will most probably have no ongoing relationship, I just say four without giving further details.

Another struggle, in the early times, was signing birthday and Christmas cards. The first year or two were the worst. I desperately wanted to write Simone's name alongside my other children. It didn't feel right to not include her. The only thing that stopped me was my concern that people would think I was delusional. In my heart and mind, Simone would have wanted to express her love and best wishes along with the rest of her family. Just because she was no longer living didn't mean she no longer cared.

I've never had a problem with talking about Simone. I know there are many people who struggle to even mention the name of the person they have lost. They prefer not to talk about the person. But, for me, it has been hugely important; for me, it's almost impossible *not* to talk about Simone. I want to keep her memory alive. I don't want my children or my wider family to struggle in mentioning Simone's name or discussing stories about her. Neither do I want her friends – from school, church or university – to forget her, so I openly talk about her. I talk about her at our family dinner table, when spending time with family and friends, at church, or whenever a memory of Simone comes to mind. I have always encouraged my children to do likewise, to not feel awkward or restricted about mentioning Simone's name. I have continued to post photos and a statement on Facebook about

Simone every year, on her birthday and anniversary. While some may see this as a request for sympathy, that is not my intention. I simply want Simone to be remembered.

I have been guided in this by what a friend told me, many years ago, when her brother died in a car accident. She said that she hated it when people would not talk about her brother for fear of hurting her. She emphasised how important it was – for her – to talk about and remember her brother. At the time, I hadn't experienced significant loss, and I was surprised. Yet this became a principle that I consciously practised when learning of another's loss, after checking first that they felt comfortable about talking freely. I would ask about their loved one, about who they were and what they were like.

I didn't really understand the truth of it, though, until those early times after losing Simone. When people didn't mention Simone's name or ask me how I was feeling, or even just give me a pat on the arm or a hug to express their sympathy, I would feel quite upset. It felt to me as though they didn't care enough. These people may have assumed that it would be difficult for me to talk about Simone, but it was the opposite. Most of the time I wanted to talk about Simone; it hurt not to talk about her. When people didn't ask, especially people with whom I was close or had some relationship, I felt hurt.

An ongoing issue for me, after losing Simone, was the fear that this could happen again, that I would lose another child, if not in a car accident, then in some other way. It started with Daniel, because he was the next eldest and my only other child who could drive, back then. I would be okay until around the time when I expected him home. Then, if he didn't return home within the next five minutes, it would begin. I would start checking out the windows, then walk onto the deck and look for his car. I would try to distract myself, but the longer it took for him to come home, the more anxious I became. My stomach would start to quake and my heart would pound fast. Various scenarios would play out in my mind, both positive and negative. I would think of all the obvious, practical reasons why he was probably late. But, against my will, frightening images would start to form in my head. Visions of car accidents would emerge. I would look out the window, return to what I was doing, then check the window again. I had to physically restrain myself from calling or texting him. If it reached the twenty-minute mark – half an hour was too much – I would have to send him a text to check that he was okay. And then I'd wait anxiously until a response came.

It didn't help that he was also travelling to the University of Wollongong. Tony and I had requested that he travel by train to the university, which he had been happy to go along with. So, he would drive to Waterfall, a twenty-minute trip, and catch the train from there. But there would be times when he needed to drive to Wollongong, to drop off an assignment or attend to a short errand.

My fear was not restricted to car accidents. I would envision all kinds of scenarios: Daniel, suffering a king hit by a group of thugs; Daniel, being attacked on the train coming home (late at night); Daniel, being robbed at knifepoint. Nightmare scenarios, of the kind we are bombarded with by media outlets.

I instituted a practice among my children that they had to text me if they were going to be late home, for any reason. This could be coming home late from school, or a school excursion, or church, or a night out with friends. The kids understood my fear. And they were, mostly, really good about complying. But they all have some of the symptoms of ADHD, especially forgetfulness and distraction. They didn't mean to forget, but they would become caught up, forget the time or, sometimes, forget their phone – something I usually don't let them leave home without!

Others' reassurances that I could not experience the loss of two children meant nothing. I have a friend who has essentially lost two children – one died due to a brain tumour, the other survived after a pedestrian accident, but her traumatic brain injury has severely impacted her life. Another woman I know has lost three of her four children to various health issues. I thought of Sophie Delezio, who was the victim of two car accidents. It could happen. It had happened to me once. It could happen again.

What about your faith, you might ask. Sadly, my faith hadn't prevented Simone from dying, and I knew from my experiences at Lifeline and through other counselling settings that being a good person does not prevent bad things from happening. As my good friend Libby, a staunch woman of faith, says, the accident could just as easily have happened to one of her three daughters.

Once Laura started going out more – not only driving, but social activities as well – my anxiety increased again because I felt that girls were more vulnerable to potential dangers. Laura is also my only daughter now, which makes her doubly precious. And we really 'get' each other. I consider her my best friend as well as my daughter. Whenever I consider the horrible possibility of losing Laura, I am shattered by the mere thought of it.

I would like to be able to say that this problem has completely disappeared, but that wouldn't be honest. I can say that I worry a lot less, though. It takes longer for me to start becoming anxious. Instead of five minutes, it will now be more like twenty or thirty minutes before I start to experience physical symptoms. My kids have also become better at letting me know when they are going to be late. I have learnt to live with it, and to be compassionate to myself because I know that my fear comes from a very real place.

Another fear that emerged as my kids became older was that they would not live beyond their twenty-first birthday. I had this horrible paranoia that my kids were not meant to reach maturity. As Daniel's twenty-first approached, I was conscious of this underlying fear. But I couldn't tell anyone. I was afraid that verbalising it would make it a reality. How crazy does that sound? Later, I learnt that Daniel and Laura had the same fear. It came up one time when we were talking about birthdays. That made me feel less crazy. I am happy to report that (at the time of publication) Daniel is thirty-one, Laura is twenty-seven and Matthew is twenty-three. That particular fear has been crushed.

I cannot speak about our loss without paying homage to the incredible support that our family received from so many people in our lives, including those we knew well and those we didn't know at all. The phone hardly stopped ringing the first few weeks, and there was an almost continual flow of visitors. This included not only our families and close friends, but also our church family, pastors and congregation members; colleagues, from past and current workplaces; neighbours, both past and present; acquaintances, both past and current. It was amazing.

We were abundantly blessed with meals, food baskets, food hampers, grocery shopping, flowers and formal floral arrangements by the dozen, letters, emails, Facebook messages, sympathy cards, books and gifts. This benevolence spread beyond days, to weeks and even many months after the accident.

My closest friends visited me often – or called me, or asked me out, or did anything I needed. My dear friend Di did my ironing for the first few weeks – maybe months – it's hard to remember now. Practical love in action. My friends cooked dinners, hung washing, fielded phone calls and made endless cups of tea. I feel fortunate to have so many wonderful people in my life.

Many people find attending a support group such as The Compassionate Friends* to be helpful. I was surrounded by so many friends and colleagues who are counsellors – in addition to having my own counsellor – that I didn't use that service, and Tony was not interested. I have been helped abundantly over the past fourteen years by friends and colleagues, and also by the staff at Anglicare, Relationships Australia, Hopefield and Catholic Care, and I will always be grateful for their support.

Over the years, we have continued to receive much love and support in so many ways. Every birthday and anniversary I receive flowers, or heartfelt texts, or Facebook messages of support, or cards from those who make a point of remembering Simone and our family. There is a strong core of support from those who are closest to us. The amount has receded, as the years go by, which is to be expected. But I will be forever grateful.

Knowing that Simone won't be forgotten is the most important thing for all of us.

In relation to returning to work – for me, and I know this is different for everyone – I couldn't see how spending more time at home grieving Simone was going to help. At that time, I was really stuck in my grief. I was at the numb, I-don't-know-what-I-am feeling thinking

---

* The Compassionate Friends is a worldwide not-for-profit organisation with local support groups that provide friendship, understanding, grief education and hope to families who have experienced child bereavement.

or doing stage. I was impatient with staying at home and 'doing nothing'. Grieving did not have a to-do list and, without one, I was at a loss. I wasn't ready to do the hard work of grief – the feeling, experiencing work. I have always been very task-oriented, and when I am not achieving, I become bored and restless. I reasoned that it would be better to return to work and at least try to help other people.

Why this stubborn determination? My thinking at the time went something like this: *I finally have the job I've always wanted, the sort of job I wanted when I left school. It has taken me nearly thirty years to finally achieve this. I can't jeopardise the job that I have always wanted. So, I'll just have to go back to work.*

The following year I began postgraduate studies in counselling at the Annandale Institute for Emotionally Focused Therapy. I know, what was I thinking? Something like this: *I was planning to start this course before Simone died. I really want to do it. Now. I can't wait. I am struggling at work, I don't have enough knowledge and skills to do this job the way I want to. I need to know everything now, preferably yesterday. I have to study more; otherwise, I can't be the best counsellor I need to be.*

How do I know now that it was too early to go back to work? With the benefit of hindsight, I can see that I was in an almost constant state of emotional turmoil. Not too many people would have known – or so I thought – because I kept it pretty well hidden except from Tony, my close friends and my therapist. But, over time, my supervisor and colleagues at Anglicare would have known. I didn't know they knew. They kept contextualising my struggles in the light of losing Simone. I didn't agree. The problem was not my grief. The problem was – you guessed it – I was not good enough!

I was easily tipped over the edge into reactivity in work with my clients and the not-good-enough story was in full swing. Now I was not only a not-good-enough mother, but also a not-good-enough counsellor. My self-criticism reached an all-time high, and although my wise and caring supervisor and my colleagues tried to encourage me, and reason with me that a lot of my reactivity was due to grief about Simone, I refused to believe them. I would pretend to agree. 'Yes, yes, you're right. Of course, that would explain it,' I would say, but in my heart, I didn't believe a word they said.

That took many more years.

CHAPTER 16

'GETTING OVER IT'

Some people don't understand big grief. They don't realise that grief has its own timetable and cannot be dictated by what others anticipate or expect. Through my grief journey, I was hurt by others who thought that I was 'stuck' in my grief, that I should be feeling better by now, that I should be 'over' my grief by now, that I 'should be coping'. Those who thought that I should 'get over it'. These are generally people who have not experienced significant loss. Grief literature speaks about the life-altering nature of child loss. The truth is that grief after the loss of your child will remain with you for the rest of your life; you'll just learn to live alongside it.

As the years passed, people tried to comfort and reassure me, saying that as time went by I (or we) would recover and the grief would ease. I didn't find this comforting; I didn't want my grief to ease. It felt to me as though lessening my grief would diminish my connection with Simone. My grief was a direct conduit to my daughter. Karen Katafiasz reframes this inner sanctum between the bereaved and their beloved in her quaint little book, *Grief Therapy*.[27] She suggests that our ongoing feelings of grief may be one of God's ways of nourishing our ongoing interconnection. I found her words to be a priceless source of affirmation.

I now know that we never lose our connection to one we have loved and lost. They remain forever in our hearts, as constant as our love for them. A beautiful children's picture book by Patrice Karst[28] speaks of the transcendent power of the invisible string that is love – it connects from our heart to the hearts of those we love, wherever they may be, whether they are on mountain tops or in the depths of the ocean or in heaven. Sometimes we need to tug on that invisible string to feel the loving connection between us. I think that image captures it well.

It took me and my family about five years to be ready to go through Simone's room and sort through her belongings. The impetus was how messy her room had become. Over the intervening years, whenever we didn't have space to store an object, it would end up in Simone's room. This didn't feel respectful to Simone's memory, and I felt embarrassed and ashamed of what her room had become. I had a vision of creating a sacred space, dedicated to all things Simone. A place where we could hang her drawings and paintings, and display her keepsakes and special mementos from her life. A place we could go to remember Simone, where our family and friends could gather and reminisce.

Laura and I did the majority of the sorting and decision-making. It was a massive undertaking that took many weeks. We figured out what we wanted to keep – paintings, artworks, clothes, jewellery and personal mementos that we could not part with. We offered some of Simone's favourite clothing items to her close friends; other clothes were given away to charities. It was emotionally gruelling work, especially sorting through her book work, her notes and a multitude of journals and handwritten prayers to God. I am glad that we waited until we were ready, as it was not a task for the faint-hearted. To do this mammoth task alongside Laura created a tangible bond of connection, both with each other and with Simone. After many weeks, the room was ready for its new purpose.

Sadly, Tony did not agree with my concept for Simone's room. He was concerned with practicality, pointing out that Daniel would benefit from having a larger room. It took me many months to get my head around this idea because I had treasured my idea for her room for so long. However, I started to think of other ways that we could celebrate Simone. We hung her artworks in our living room and in the corridor to her room. Her clothes, jewellery and other mementos were stored in a chest of drawers. And a new idea started to form in my mind, a more effective and far-reaching way of remembering and celebrating Simone. I began to ponder the idea of writing this book – a bigger, broader and, hopefully, more valuable way to share Simone's life.

So, we painted the walls and stripped back the floorboards, and Simone's old room became Daniel's. I asked Daniel how it felt for him to move into her old room; he said that the anticipation of moving into her room was the hardest part. He was worried that he would be too sad and assailed with memories of Simone to be able to make her room feel like his own. However, once we had removed everything from her room and had it repainted and recarpeted, it felt like a new space for him, and he no longer struggled with the difficult emotions of taking over her bedroom.

After Daniel married Bella and moved out of home, Daniel's room, previously Simone's room, became my home office, the room where I have been writing this book. It has been a healing experience to be writing about Simone in her old room. It feels right and fitting to be remembering, reading and writing about her in this space. And instead of having a Simone museum, I have created a book about Simone. On my desk is the rosewood box with Simone's ashes, and Simone's face gazes out at me. She looks so peaceful and content. I have a memory box that I created at a grief workshop on the bookcase behind me, which holds some precious items: photos; a lock of Simone's hair; some knitting from the scarf she was working on; a cutting from her painting jeans; her favourite red wallet; her headband; her pink beanie; her school medal for Visual Arts; paintbrushes; sand and shells to celebrate her love of the beach; some of her handwritten notes; and some pieces of beaded jewellery that she made.

Spring is the celebration of new life, but, for us, each September marks the memory of losing Simone. As the weather becomes warmer and the jasmine near our front doorway blooms with its sweet nectar, as the dragonflies gather around the spring blooms, a bittersweet sadness fills my heart.

One of the many challenges I still struggle with is dealing with life events that Simone will never experience. Each time one of her friends becomes engaged, and then married, and then becomes a mother, I can't help feeling sad, and envious on behalf of Simone. It's particularly difficult with the friends that Simone grew up with, from her early school years. I have worked hard not to give in to feelings of resentment and bitterness, but instead focus on my happiness for these girls. It has been tough going at times.

None of these feelings were present, however, when we were blessed to share in Erica's wedding, a year or so after Simone died. This was a truly joyous and very special wedding celebration. Erica was kind enough to acknowledge Simone's absence, and our presence, at her wedding with genuine, heartfelt sentiments. I felt able to fully enjoy and participate in the wedding day, though of course I felt sadness that Simone was not there to be part of the occasion.

The wedding of my long-time bachelor brother John – at the ripe old age of forty-six – was another time where I experienced bittersweet feelings. While I was extremely happy for him to begin a life of married bliss, I felt a lot of sadness that Mum, Simone and Danny were not physically present at this significant life event. I knew, without any shadow of a doubt, how happy Mum, Danny and Simone would have been for John to find love and marriage. And while I knew they were all present in spirit during the service, I couldn't help lamenting the loss of their physical presence.

I was asked to say a special prayer during the church service, in honour of those who had died. This was tough. I shed some tears, but somehow managed to hold it together and make it through. Later, during the wedding reception, I was pleased to give a speech in honour of the happy couple. This was a lot easier than during the peak of emotions provoked by the church service.

In more recent years, we have had the joyful experience of adding, instead of losing, family members. We watched with interest and happiness as Daniel's friendship with Bella grew into love, engagement and then a wedding, more than seven years ago now. This has been such a joy for our family. Now there is new life. Daniel and Bella were blessed with the birth of a son, Gabriel, in October 2018. My first grandchild! And Sebastian followed in September 2020.

While I have felt much joy in the celebration of love and new life, it is mingled with sorrow, as Simone hasn't had the opportunity to share the blossoming of Daniel's relationship, come to know Bella or to meet her nephews. Curiously, Bella has a lot in common with Simone, and I think they would have connected well with each other. Bella is also a schoolteacher, has a strong and passionate Christian faith and loves reading. Bella has agreed that they would have been great friends as well as sisters-in-law.

Laura also married her childhood sweetheart, in July four years ago. This is another relationship that Simone has not been there to witness and enjoy. Laura has told me over the years of her own sorrows of not having her older sister by her side – to confide in, share experiences with, laugh, love and enjoy life. While Simone knew Kieran a little from our family friendship with his family, she never had the opportunity to be part of his life journey, as he went through school, dated and then married Laura, and became part of our family.

I have felt heartbroken, at times, about Simone's absence at the weddings of her brother and sister. She would have made a beautiful and joyous bridesmaid (and bride). This has been part of my experience of grief, big grief. And while Laura's and Daniel's weddings were occasions of great joy and celebration, they were tinged with the pain of a wedding party that was incomplete.

CHAPTER 17

WHAT I HAVE LEARNT ABOUT MENTAL HEALTH

I believe that the emotional wellbeing journey continues throughout a lifetime. I don't know if we ever arrive at a place of total healing, at least not on this side of heaven. I do believe, however, that each day provides a new opportunity to learn, to grow, to heal, and to become a more integrated, loving and accepting human being.

I have learnt so much from my experiences – about matters that I wouldn't have understood without my struggles. Yet studying and practising in the area of mental health has also been part of my journey. I have written this chapter to provide an introduction to some of the mental health issues that I have discussed. It is different from the rest of the book, as it touches on the theory, in order to add academic rigour to these topics. While I refer to my personal experience to provide context, I hope that it also provides a deeper understanding of these subjects. I have provided attribution for all sources, in case you would like to do further reading.

I have also subdivided this chapter into sections, with subheadings listed alphabetically, for ease of use.

About ADHD

ADHD is a big, complex subject. There is much I would like to share about this disorder because it has had a significant impact on my life and the lives of my children, especially Simone. Due to its complexity, however, I can't do justice to the topic in the space I have available, so I will simply cover a few important points.

ADHD is a contentious issue. Even today, when extensive evidence supports its existence, there are unbelievers, both among professionals and in the wider community. Yet ADHD, especially undiagnosed ADHD, has a huge impact on the lives of girls and women, and leads to a multiplicity of mental health issues, including, but not limited to, depression, anxiety, eating disorders and self-image struggles. Its effects include disorganisation, emotional reactivity, underachievement, low self-esteem and impaired relationships. The inattentive form of ADHD is most common among girls and women, yet it is the least understood and identified form, thus the least diagnosed. This is due, at least in part, to the vast difference in presentation of ADHD in females, as opposed to males. This has been established and corroborated by experts in the field.[29]

An important secondary consequence of ADHD is the impact on a young woman's developing self-image, which has been vividly described by Sari Solden.[30] These young women will ask themselves questions such as, 'What is wrong with me?' They commonly describe themselves as incompetent, immature or feeling like an impostor. There are many culturally inscribed messages that are inflicted on women as they mature, and if there are struggles to meet them, it can cause strong feelings of shame and guilt. It is often difficult for women with ADHD to cope with the multiple and conflicting demands of being women – as wives, mothers, in the workplace and in society more generally. This can lead to women having a chronic sense of underachievement, a depressed mood, and to feeling overwhelmed and overworked. The negative self-talk can become incessant, leading to the development of depression.

These secondary consequences of ADHD mirror my life experiences – the emotional torment I have wrestled with – as described earlier. It has been further complicated by the fact that at times I forget or minimise the impact of ADHD on many of my inadequacies. I have often rationalised and judged my ADHD traits as not being that bad, reasoning that I have mild symptoms of ADHD.

There is also the issue of ADHD mothers parenting ADHD children. Sari Solden[31] explains that mothers with ADHD have additional struggles parenting children with ADHD. Research by Kathleen G. Nadeau, Ellen B. Littman and Patricia O. Quinn[32] maintains that the parents of girls with ADHD have a tendency to feel more overwhelmed by their parenting role, experiencing higher stress and frustration levels. They have also shown that there is a strong tendency for parents to be critical and intrusive, with high levels of expressed emotion, vacillating between frustration and anxiety in response to their daughter's behaviours. Mothers can be ambivalent, enmeshed and overinvolved, which sometimes leads to toxic mother–daughter relationships.

About anger

Anger is an emotion that is often disparaged or maligned but, like all emotions, it has both positive and negative elements. Anger, when it is out of control and expressed aggressively, can be a dangerous emotion, yet anger can also be a valuable life tool. Our feelings of anger communicate that something is not right. It is a signal that we, or someone we care about, is being treated unfairly, or that important personal boundaries have been crossed.

The most important consideration about anger is how we manage it. As Aristotle states in *The Art of Rhetoric*, 'Anyone can become angry – that is easy, but to be angry with the right person, to the right degree, at the right time, for the right purpose and in the right way – that is not easy.'[33]

Over the years, through my battles with anger, I have learnt some helpful concepts. I found Stephanie Dowrick's writings on the subject to be wise, sensitive, and written in a way that made me feel understood and offered ideas that I could take on board. In *The Universal Heart*,[34] she reminded me that I always have a choice about how I respond in any given situation, whether with anger or with self-control. That in the vital split second of hesitation before I act, I have a choice about how I respond. It's important to take a brief pause and remember that some issues are worth fighting for and some are not. She suggests asking yourself whether or not it is worth it in this instance, and what might be a more helpful way to respond. She reminds us that if we are in a loving relationship but are also aggressive, having the intention to stop being angry is not enough; our actions need to reflect our loving intentions. We can't be distracted by our own excuses because we are not helpless victims.

Harriet Lerner is a psychotherapist who has written a classic book, *The Dance of Anger*.[35] She asks pertinent questions about what our anger boils down to, whose issue it is really, and how we can respond differently. She also suggests that openly expressing anger often perpetuates unhealthy patterns in relationships and generally doesn't lead to the changes we desire.

Applying these principles requires significant effort; it is much easier to react in a familiar angry or defensive way. But if I really want to manage my anger and become the person I desire to be, I need to remember that I have a choice in how I respond. I wonder if you can relate to this scenario. You've had a stressful afternoon and are cooking dinner while supervising your kids, who are not doing their homework. Instead, they're teasing their siblings and are basically getting on your nerves. You lose it, you shout, you demand that they shut up and do their homework. Suddenly, the phone rings.

It is your best friend, calling to ask you a favour. Do you shout in irritation because she has interrupted your cooking? No. If you are like me, you don't because you value and care for your friend. So, you stop, take a breath and speak to them warmly and kindly. How can I do this for my friend, but not my children, who were also interrupting my dinner preparations? Of course, it's partly a matter of societal norms – we don't usually shout at our adult friends – and I feel a sense of responsibility about my children doing their homework. Yet I also know that I have *chosen* to respond differently because I stopped and thought. In this instance, I have exercised restraint and made a conscious decision about how I responded. A problem I had with my children was that often I didn't stop and think before I opened my mouth.

While these books were helpful, I spent many years trying to fix my anger without understanding or dealing with its sources. I have now learnt that I need to attend to my anger. I need to identify *that* I feel angry, understand *why* I feel angry and consider the deeper underlying feelings that are fuelling my anger in this instance.

Certainly, over the course of my life, a lot of my anger was directed at myself – and anger turned inwards becomes depression. But I also projected a lot of anger onto Simone. The sources of my anger were a complex mixture of thoughts and emotions. Some of my anger at Simone was for the traits that I disliked in myself, especially those from childhood. As a parent, I was trying to help her, to shape and guide her so that she wouldn't experience the same suffering as I did. My intentions were good, but the execution of this guidance was problematic, especially when I was frustrated or stressed. This angry dynamic, once entrenched, is very difficult to change. I know this now. Working with other's experiences of anger in relationships has helped me to develop a deeper appreciation for recurring patterns in relationships, and how impervious they are to change. They require sustained effort and determination, qualities that were difficult for me to achieve when I was feeling overwhelmed by raising four children.

The theory about anger is that it is often a secondary emotion, although it can also be a primary one. Primary feelings are natural and instinctive. They always come first, but may move through us quickly, sometimes outside our conscious awareness. Primary emotions are fundamental, adaptive and move us towards action. These feelings are evolutionary, developing in response to survival. Underneath secondary anger may be a primary feeling of fear, shame, grief, hurt or rejection. Or various gradations of these feelings, such as dread, unhappiness, irritation, embarrassment, disappointment or some combination of them. Secondary emotions operate protectively and defensively. They act in a controlling way (beyond our consciousness), obscuring the primary emotion, often with another emotion that we feel able to express. For instance, within our family of origin, sadness may be acceptable, while anger is not. Confusion or anxiety are often ways in which secondary emotions will present. A good metaphor for this experience is an iceberg. What is visible – the top of the iceberg peeking out of the water, or the secondary emotion, the reaction – doesn't include the rest of the iceberg, the primary emotion, hidden in the depths. Or the anger itself may be primary when someone has wronged or hurt us.

Whether primary or secondary, our anger is always a sign that something is wrong. Anger serves an important purpose, to alert us when we have been treated unfairly or unkindly. Unfortunately, we have been raised to believe that our anger is bad: shameful, sinful. Especially for girls. 'Nice girls don't get angry.' Boys almost seem to have permission to be angry, giving rise to clichéd sayings, such as 'Boys will be boys' or 'Just let them fight it out'.

Yet anger is only bad when it hurts others or when it is expressed in an abusive way – verbally, emotionally or physically, through violence and/or coercive control. Anger that is expressed assertively helps us to be heard and understood, and acknowledges our individual perspective and our experience.

So, how do we manage our feelings of anger and express them assertively? The theory of emotionally focused therapy (EFT)[36] maintains that blocking our anger leads to acting out with defence mechanisms, such as blaming, controlling and other forms of emotional reactivity. When we do this, we don't reach the heart of the issue, the primary anger. Instead, our secondary anger is expressed in dysfunctional ways, which cause problems in our life.

What we need is to be able to identify, express and experience our anger in the therapeutic presence of a safe other: a partner or a close and trusted friend, or what Alice Miller calls 'the enlightened witness',[37] such as a therapist. Releasing anger in this way not only is cathartic, but also exposes the primary emotions that are sitting beneath the anger, often outside of our conscious awareness. When we are free to express these primary feelings, we experience a sense of freedom, of letting go of a burden that we have been carrying. It also frees us to be our authentic, genuine self.

An example of this in my life was the anger I felt towards Dad after the loss of Mum and Simone. I often felt let down by him, and that I wasn't important to him. This anger simmered away for a long time, erupting now and then when something about our relationship triggered me strongly. It wasn't until I was able to freely express my anger, in the safe, non-judgemental presence of my therapist, that I was overwhelmed by an immense feeling of grief. I was suddenly caught in a vortex of gut-searing anguish, and I couldn't stop crying. I discovered that grief had been fuelling the anger towards my dad, and I'd had no idea.

Once I was able to express my anger and experience sadness and grief, the rage and fury towards my dad evaporated. I may have felt disappointed at times but, for the most part, I accepted him as he is.

As anger generates a lot of energy, there are actions that we can take to moderate our anger. In the case of overwhelming anger that hits us without notice, it is more effective to find safe ways of physically expressing anger, such as through exercise – jogging or running, tearing up old newspapers, stamping feet, hitting a punching bag, going outside and taking out your anger on an inanimate object. These methods enable us to safely release our anger without hurting others and, ultimately, not hurting ourselves. What I learnt about my anger with Dad and Simone was that projecting my anger onto them not only hurt them, but also hurt me.

Stephanie Dowrick talks a lot about the value of self-awareness for all aspects of managing our emotions, especially in the most important aspect of our lives, our relationships. For it is in our relationships that we learn and grow the most. I thoroughly recommend reading Stephanie's classic work, *Intimacy & Solitude*,[38] to understand this more fully.

For further insight into women's anger and relationships, read Harriet Lerner's bestselling book, *The Dance of Anger*.[35] I have found all of Harriet's books that focus on the 'dance' in relationships to have been invaluable sources of knowledge.

About anxiety

It is important to understand that we all have the propensity for anxiety, due to our biology and our neurological wiring. Experiences of nervousness and worry are uncomfortable, but they serve the important purpose of keeping us safe. In Australia, anxiety-related conditions are the most common mental health disorder, affecting approximately fourteen per cent of the population. As that is only the proportion that are reported, the real number is likely much higher.

Anxiety affects the whole body; its impact is felt physically, intellectually, emotionally and behaviourally. Psychologists speak of three major groups of anxiety: panic disorder, generalised anxiety disorder and social anxiety disorder. Each one has different symptoms and effects, and they often go hand in hand with depression.

A lot has been written about anxiety, its antecedents and its impact on life. Personally, I like how Bev Aisbett, cartoonist and anxiety sufferer, has simply but effectively described her experiences in cartoons with captions. She comments, rightly in my opinion, that anxiety is caused by being out of balance – not taking care of our physical, intellectual, emotional and spiritual wellbeing – for many years.[39] One of the most important lessons I have learnt is the need to keep my life in balance. A healthy state of equilibrium will differ for each of us. Age, gender, your health profile, personality, extroversion or introversion will all be influential factors. Finding your own sense of balance is vitally important for managing your mental health.

The triggers that lead to being out of balance relate to both the personal (our childhood, temperament, ability to express how we are feeling, whether we are self- or other critical, a worrier or more laid-back) and the experiential (pressured/stressed lifestyle, due to workplace or home life; the drive for perfection; fear of or focus on failure or making mistakes; a negative perspective on life; comparing yourself to others; feeling responsible for others' feelings). As Bev Aisbett rightly points out, all these attributes are based on fear. Fear of being judged unworthy, being disapproved of, not belonging, being vulnerable, being rejected, not being loved, even fear of fear.

Another consequence of anxiety is that giving in to anxiety leads to feelings of hopelessness and powerlessness. For me, this increases my sense of incompetency and inadequacy, making me unwilling to try activities outside my comfort zone. This keeps me locked into a vicious cycle. Until you challenge yourself, you cannot prove to yourself that you have the ability to succeed. It is by giving things a go, trying and failing, and being prepared to try again, that confidence and self-esteem are built.

Fortunately, in recent times, people have been coming out of the fear closet and opening up about their experiences of anxiety. An excellent account of this is in Sarah Wilson's honest and eloquent book, *First, We Make the Beast Beautiful*,[40] a powerful story about her battles with anxiety and mental health. It is important and liberating for other anxiety sufferers to know that people are willing to describe their own struggles. This helps to normalise and lessen the stigma of anxiety and other mental health conditions.

Severe anxiety and/or panic attacks are absolutely the pits. Psychologist Margaret Wehrenberg, who works with anxiety sufferers, says that a common refrain is, 'I don't think I want to live if I have to go on feeling like this.'[41] I totally relate to this sentiment. As someone who has lived with anxiety, day in and day out – especially at those times when it has escalated to panic attacks – I can attest that the anxious life is hardly worth living.

I have been diagnosed with generalised anxiety disorder, but I have also experienced panic attacks. For most people with panic disorder, the fear of having another panic attack increases the likelihood of having another, as fear breeds panic. After a particularly severe panic attack, I sought advice from a counsellor, I read up on panic attacks, and whenever I felt the signs of panic growing within me (racing thoughts, racing heart, sweating, confused and irrational thinking) I would speak calmly to myself, I would sit in the sun and meditate, or I would call Tony or a friend and speak logically and calmly with them. My panic attacks have decreased now and, fortunately, I know what to do if I feel the signs.

What I have learnt, from that experience and others, is to not avoid or distract myself from my anxious feelings. That doesn't mean that I launch into them head-on, but I have discovered that avoiding my feelings makes my panic worse. I need to face my fears calmly and logically; I talk to myself gently and rationally. I start to breathe mindfully and to meditate if possible. If I am too emotionally affected, I will speak to someone I trust. I need to break my connection with the racing thoughts, to disengage and disconnect from them, and these strategies help me to have power over them.

About depression
I remember the day when it finally dawned on me that I had been suffering from depression for most of my life. I was forty-two at the

time. I was attending a professional development training day where Matthew Johnstone was speaking about his experiences with depression. Matthew has written and illustrated a series of books about the black dog of depression that has plagued him throughout his life. When I read his simple but evocative book, *I Had a Black Dog*,[42] I recognised my own experiences in the illustrations and their captions. I realised that I had been depressed since I was a young child and could relate to all the symptoms and their long-term impact on my life. It was a revelation! I can't believe that it took me so long to work out that depression was not just a casual on/off visitor but a consistent and endogenous part of my life.

I came to realise that the postnatal depression I suffered after the birth of my four children was simply a ramping up of symptoms that were there all the time. Strangely, it was a consolation to understand that it was the black dog of depression that had impacted my life experiences so severely. It helped me to have an explanation that described what was continually happening in my life.

Depression can be likened to living on an emotional rollercoaster. When a close friend would ask me how I was travelling, I would often say 'somewhere on the emotional rollercoaster'. It was a shorthand way of explaining that I was caught on the depression train. I relate strongly to Allison Mierop's articulation of her experience of depression.[43] She describes periods of relief when the depression has slowed down or receded. At other times, there may be a sense of barely getting by, while there will also be times of going up the incline, travelling fast, with scared, anxious thoughts and feelings. It is a rollercoaster ride that you can't seem to get off, as much as you want to or try to.

My experience of depression was dominated by intense feelings of mental, physical and emotional exhaustion. It was so draining. Tiredness is now my early warning sign that depression is hovering somewhere in the wings of my emotional experience.

Depression stole so many years of my life. It eroded my happiness, confidence, self-esteem and especially any sense of inner peace. Inside, there was only torment, pain and misery. Depression sucked all of the joy out of life. I find Dorothy Rowe's description of depression to be particularly apt. She describes depression as an entirely different experience from unhappiness. When we are unhappy, we can be comforted by others and, importantly, we can give ourselves kindness and compassion. But when we are depressed, we cannot be cheered up, especially not by ourselves. We feel as though we are the problem and we don't deserve to be happy. She talks about depression being an impermeable barrier that nothing external can pass through.[44]

I can totally relate to this. While my experiences of grief have been gut-wrenching and painful, they have not affected me the same way that my battles with depression have. It is difficult to understand unless you have experienced depression yourself, but depression has plummeted me to unfathomable depths.

In my experiences of grief, I have found comfort in the presence and support of friends and loved ones. When I am depressed, I feel no hope for myself or my future, and there is little that can soothe the pain within. Only I can do that. Yet, when I am depressed, I don't have the energy, resources, strength or even the willingness to do it.

During my therapy studies, I became aware of an image that visually described my inner emotional experience. I drew a large heart. Surrounding my heart, I drew a thick black outline to represent the dense rubber-like wall that protects my vulnerable, wounded child self* but also prevents external sources of help from penetrating. I realised that the rubber-like wall was maintained (and had been constructed) by a mixture of Mum's words and my inner critic. I thought I needed it to protect myself, and maybe I did, but it also trapped me inside and prevented me from healing and changing.

Dorothy Rowe sees the prison of depression as a personal construct. It sounds harsh, but her reasoning makes sense in relation to my image. It can take a long time, however, for us to realise that we are the only one who has the key to the prison door. It took me many years to realise that. If a therapist had told me that I was causing my own depression in my early years of therapy, I would have been angry and indignant. I would have pointed out that I hated being depressed, and that I would never choose to be depressed.

Dorothy Rowe also links depression to a core belief in not being good enough – a resounding belief throughout my own life.[45] Those of us who suffer from depression are in bondage to a belief that we must consistently struggle to reach a standard, one that is far above ourselves, and one that we fear we will never reach. We put enormous effort into being good, yet constantly struggle with feelings of guilt about the limitations of our success.

I learnt from my studies at the Annandale Institute for Emotionally Focused Therapy that the foundation for a belief in not being good enough comes from early childhood experience. Dr Michelle Webster, the director of the institute, explains that an abandoned emotional

---

* The wounded child is the part of the inner child that carries hurt and trauma from childhood.

pattern develops when children have not been seen or acknowledged by a parent (or parents) and they try to nurture their own parent in order to receive nurturing in return. When this doesn't occur, they end up feeling not good enough. 'They tend to wonder what is wrong with them and blame themselves that they are inadequate, or not good enough. These people tend to be very compliant, being prepared to do whatever others want in order to be good.'[46] This fits with my experience of growing up in my family. I often didn't feel seen or understood by my parents. And as my mother was frequently unwell, I worked hard to emotionally nurture her, giving her all my love, attention and focus in order to hopefully receive that nurturing in response. However, the message I received in return was that I was not good enough. Therefore, I was constantly trying to be a 'good girl', in order to win her favour and to not disappoint her.

This pattern of emotionally nurturing others, due to a belief in not being good enough, continued in my adult relationships. I often put myself to one side in order to help others, especially when I was grieving. I still strived to be the best daughter, the best friend, the best mother and the best counsellor, without taking my needs into consideration. This was exhausting and led to depression, emotional breakdown and burnout. Since reaching a place of greater understanding, I have become better at putting boundaries in place, to ensure that I don't give to a point that is detrimental to me.

About the inner critic
Believing that I was not good enough came from my inner critic. My inner critic was a crucial force that influenced all aspects of my life, particularly how I parented Simone. Only perfection was good enough. In my mind, there were no excuses for my parenting struggles.

What I learnt from therapy, however, was that I had internalised a lot of my mother's injunctions and expectations around being selfless and sacrificial. I could so often hear my mother's voice in my ear – telling me I was selfish, or lazy, or too much like my father or that I needed to try harder. All some version of not being good enough. But these messages were *not* expressed the way Mum would have said them, rather they had morphed into an ugly, twisted version of her words, which was scathing, sarcastic, nasty and heartless. This was the voice of my inner critic.

So, what is this inner critic that I keep referring to, and how can it have so much power in our lives? Hal Stone and Sidra Stone's book, *Embracing Your Inner Critic*,[47] was an invaluable tool in answering those questions for me. The inner critic develops as a reaction to our parents – and other important role models, such as teachers, relatives, pastors, mentors – and it is designed to protect us from humiliation and social stigma. Our parents (and other leaders) are teaching us how to behave appropriately in order to succeed in the world, both at home and in the workforce. To a large extent, our inner critic acts as our conscience, ensuring that we make good decisions that will help, not hinder, our lives and our relationship with others. Our inner critic serves to keep us on the 'straight and narrow' path, to ensure that we are responsible and capable. Its original intentions are designed for benefit. Unfortunately, for some of us, this inner critic goes into hyper-drive and damages us from the inside out, constantly berating us and stealing the joy from our lives.

For those raised within a religious family, the scriptural framework becomes another source of condemnation for our inner critic. We are taught an interrelated set of rules, of expectations, to live up to, standards expected by God, in order to achieve salvation and eternal life.

This combination of messages from parents and the church certainly increased the power of my inner critic. Although the message of the Christian gospel espouses God's grace – his unconditional love and acceptance through the life and death of Jesus Christ – there are also mixed messages. Reminders of God's love sit alongside reminders of God's expectations and his wrath. I felt as though I could never live up to these expectations (especially given my focus on my past failures and sins), so it was another element of not being good enough.*

My inner critic fed my guilt and shame, continually telling me that there was something wrong with me. Its constant refrain was, *'You are just not good enough. Whatever you do, you will never be good enough.'* And I believed it, one hundred per cent. I believed I was a failure, at everything I had done in my life. I felt as though FAILURE was tattooed on my forehead, along with PREY, NOT GOOD ENOUGH and INCOMPETENT. What were my sins? What were my failures?

It was not only my parenting failures, with Simone and my subsequent children, but also every aspect of my life. It was a bottomless list: my negative and judgemental thoughts; my anger; the bad decisions I had made; my inability to change, to become the parent, wife, person that I craved to be. I also condemned myself for many of the traits that are associated with ADHD, such as inconsistency, poor time management, short working memory, disorganisation, being easily distracted and having difficulties finishing what I'd started. I wanted to succeed, to be special, to be loved and to be worthwhile. To be that person, up there on the pedestal, that idealised self: the perfect mother, the perfect wife, the perfect friend, the perfect counsellor.

---

* My experiences with this in relation to faith have been greatly assisted by reading the works of Brennan Manning, who speaks evocatively about the power of the grace we find in Jesus, who offers us unconditional love and forgiveness.

The discrepancy between my ideal and my reality were too far apart, too big a chasm to bridge. Psychologists call it cognitive dissonance – feelings of unease that arise when your beliefs run counter to your behaviour.[48] Although discomfort is too mild a word to describe how I felt – anguish or torment would be more accurate.

I became aware of my inner critic through therapy, and later through reading and training, and I knew, cognitively and emotionally, how damaging it could be. Yet, I *could not* and *would not* let go of my inner critic. I believed that without it I would make more mistakes that would lead to further failure. I literally saw my inner critic as a thick black line that I must follow. I needed to stay right on track, without deviation. Without my critic I was convinced that I would stuff up.

The critic's intention is to keep you safe, to stop you from continuing to feel the pain, shame and vulnerability that you experienced as a child. This was something I learnt from my postgraduate therapy studies – when the critic is loud in our life, it is working hard to protect the vulnerable wounded child within. Hal Stone and Sidra Stone explain that when the inner critic attacks, it is basically a cry for help. It is responding to a fear that you are in danger of abandonment or rejection. The critic is born to keep us safe: my inner critic was adamant about its duty to protect the vulnerable sensitive child that I was, who continues to live inside me.[49]

Unfortunately, my critic was so virulent, so harsh, that it just kept on bashing away at my wounded, sensitive child self, thus creating a savage catch-22 cycle: instead of protecting me, it abused me. Thus, it kept me in my prison and prevented any long-lasting change from happening.

Over the years, when I would speak to my family, friends, colleagues or my therapist, each one of them would tell me that I was too hard on myself. When they did this, I thought to myself, *Yeah, I know that, everyone tells me that, but you don't understand that I cannot live without this.* I truly felt I deserved the weight of my constant criticism. I would think, *There is so much proof, so much evidence that I am not good enough, how can I deny it?* To me it felt inauthentic, dishonest and irresponsible not to believe all that I told myself.

Unfortunately, it took some time to make peace with my critic and break down the prison walls. There were breakthroughs over the years; some truths penetrated the thick shield that I'd placed around my heart. There would be moments/days/weeks/months when I would believe and have hope in myself. This may have been when a new insight or awareness came through in therapy, or when I read something in a book that resonated, or in a sermon, or a hymn, or in the words of a friend or work colleague. These include but are not limited to: when I was diagnosed with ADHD; when I realised I had clinical, endogenous depression; when I discovered the impact of trauma and abandonment; when I realised that the reason I was so hard on Simone was because of how much I loved her (that was a big one); when I received positive affirmations from friends, family, colleagues and, later, clients; when I remembered that God loved me, just as I am, through the grace of Jesus.

I have also learnt about the power of self-compassion. It is a vital and potent source of healing, and a way to work with your inner critic, rather than against it (as I had done for many years). Kristin Neff has written extensively about the power of compassion in her book, *Self-Compassion*.[50] Self-compassion differs from self-esteem: it's not an evaluation of self-worth. Instead, it's about the reality that we all have strengths and weaknesses, but these don't define us or determine our sense of worth.

The three core components of self-compassion that Neff identifies are: self-kindness, to be gentle and understanding of ourselves, rather than critical and judgemental; recognition that we are all part of a common humanity, so connection, rather than isolation and alienation, is required; and mindfulness, which is about focusing clearly on the present moment, with non-judgemental acceptance.

This third element of self-compassion really struck a chord with me. Kristin Neff speaks about this in an article she wrote for *The Self-Acceptance Project*.[51] She speaks about how the most important part of self-compassion is how we respond to our inner critic, or what she calls our 'critical voice'. Instead of becoming angry or fighting with our inner critic, we need to validate and honour what our critic is trying to tell us. As discussed, the critic's primary aim is to help us. If we can thank and appreciate the critic's efforts, it will feel heard, and then it can let go and relax. Being listened to is so important. When we feel heard, we can relax and stop fighting to prove our point, and it's exactly the same with our inner critic.

About parenting

We are fortunate, today, to live in a world that is more accepting about the struggles mothers face. In previous generations, there was little discussion about women's needs, or the plight of mothers who had trouble adapting to parenting, or who experienced postnatal depression, and they certainly weren't represented in the media. To admit, publicly, that the huge changes that come into your life through parenthood may be difficult, depressing or not enjoyable was considered shameful. This led to people hiding how they really felt, which only caused increased pressure. Not talking about our authentic experiences makes the problem worse by maintaining a false illusion.

I recently came across a book called *When Your Kids Push Your Buttons*,[52] which I have found to be one of the most helpful and supportive books about the parenting experience. It's written in the format of one mother speaking to another, a mother who understands the frustrations that parents face, and who has insight and practical solutions to help address them. It normalised my struggles with parenting, and it assisted me to feel less alone and less abnormal about the issues that I'd faced.

A phrase I had found myself saying often over the difficult years of parenting was that Simone seemed to 'push all of my buttons'. At the time, I wasn't sure exactly what it meant, though I knew that the emotions I experienced with Simone seemed to tip me over the edge. Reading what Bonnie Harris has to say about button-pushing behaviour felt akin to a soothing balm applied to a hot and painful burn. Finally, someone who *really* understood how I felt. She explains that our children are experts in pushing our buttons, in turning us into the kind of parent we spend so much time and energy fighting against becoming. Unfortunately, the angrier we become, the more our children push those buttons, creating a perpetual pattern of emotional reactivity.

How do we know when our child is pushing our buttons? It's when we experience those all-too-familiar strong emotions – in my case, rage, despair or helplessness – and we tend to react in ways that we later regret. When we are in these states, we are not reasonable; we don't make good decisions about how to handle the situation.

A significant factor in being emotionally reactive is what Bonnie calls 'automatic behaviours'. These emerge from our unconscious mind, where they have been hibernating, and are often generated when our own (buried) experiences from childhood or adolescence are reactivated. This leads us to express old frustrations and wounds that were never expressed to, or understood by, our parents. I found this explanation so helpful in understanding why I was often triggered by Simone's behaviours. Bonnie asserts that 'no parenting skills can come to the rescue of a parent whose buttons are being pushed'.[53] Wow, I knew that one, from hard-learnt experience! Hadn't I tried everything, yet nothing changed, either with my behaviour or Simone's? It was Groundhog Day, every day.

When I consider this now, with hindsight, it totally fits. I would tell Simone (multiple times) what to do and she didn't do it. She then became the unfortunate scapegoat for anger that had been building since my childhood days, which came directly from my own childhood experience of not being listened to. My anger had grown, in the depths of my being, waiting for a time when I was pushed into a corner by stress, frustration and overwhelm.

And there were probably good reasons why Simone didn't listen, but I didn't take the time to find out. I neglected to look at what might have been beneath her non-listening; instead, I took it personally, believing it to be directed at me intentionally, and I lashed out. Yet, as parents, what we need to do is to take the focus off our own agenda (in my case, my experience of not being listened to), and listen to what our child is telling us. They often can't tell us in words, so they speak to us through their behaviour; a child's behaviour is an accurate barometer of their internal emotional state.

When I think back to the interactions that commonly occurred between us during Simone's childhood, she was often telling me the same thing I was telling her, 'You are not listening to me!' However, she spoke to me through her behaviour, while I spoke through words of anger. This was beyond ironic!

Another helpful parenting book I discovered, which discusses related themes, is called *How to Talk So Kids Will Listen & Listen So Kids Will Talk*.[54] It describes the difference that occurs when we take the time to stop and really listen to what our kids are telling us. And as part of our listening process, focus specifically on the emotional experience that goes with the story. Then, in our responses, don't jump to conclusions that blame our child or make assumptions about their behaviour, but simply listen and reflect back to them what we have heard them say. It sounds simple, but is harder to practise in busy, everyday life.

What was demonstrated was that when a parent focused on just listening and reflecting back in short empathic statements what they heard, the results were vastly different to what they experienced when they listened and responded in their usual way.

While I always intended to listen to my children's stories about what happened to them at school or in the playground with friends, or later in their teen years, sometimes I mentally switched off. Usually I would be cooking dinner, tidying the house, whatever it was and I would listen with half an ear. I would assume that I knew what they were talking about or what the problem was, thinking it was some version of what I had heard before. But, of course, that is not always the case. My children deserved to be listened to with my full attention, respect and concentration, the same attention that I would give a friend who called or my husband when he came home from work.

Other times I might make an assumption about what I supposed or guessed the problem to be. For example, 'Are you sure that you listened to the teacher properly about what you were meant to be doing in your science project, you know how you tune out sometimes?' or 'Did you do that deliberately because your feelings were hurt, the same way you did with your brother the other day?' You get the basic idea here. I jumped to conclusions based on what I perceived to be my child's weaknesses or flaws, which may or may not have been part of the problem. And even if they were part of the problem, it was more important for me to be on my kid's side, not against them. I need to be their best ally, not their enemy, suspecting them of foul play.

There are many other great books about parenting, and I have listed some of them in my Recommended Reading List. However, the most painful and most effective parenting lesson I received was losing Simone. Suddenly, I understood that I needed to *really* listen to what my children were saying, both through their words and through their actions. I needed to accept that I would never be a perfect parent, but that I could learn how to be a 'good enough' parent.* Instead of being reactive and upset by what my children said or did that worried, hurt or offended me, I needed to stop and listen before I responded. I would remind myself, 'I need to do things differently than I did with Simone. I may only have this one chance, right now, to respond in a more loving, accepting way.'

So, when Laura talks (and she talks a lot!), I listen. I put aside what I am doing. I make time to be with her. And when she tells me that I have said or done something that is wrong in her eyes, for whatever reason, instead of being reactive, I take it in quietly and sit with it. I ask myself if what she is saying fits my words and behaviour. If it does, I take it on board. I don't argue with her, or become defensive; I accept it as a learning experience. If Laura needs me, I make sure that I am there for her. If she is upset, I listen first, and I ask what she thinks second. And I advise last.

---

* This is a term coined by Dr Donald Winnicott, paediatrician and psychoanalyst, who asserts that the adaptive healthiness of the 'good enough' mother (in contrast to the 'perfect' mother) is sufficient to meet a child's needs.

The importance of self-care

One of the most valuable lessons I have learnt is the importance of self-care. Each one of us possesses a lifelong need for self-care, as it helps us to balance the various challenges in our lives. I think that this is especially the case for mothers. And, at times, the care for yourself needs to come first. You may be familiar with the analogy about parents needing to put their oxygen mask on first before they attend to their children's masks on an airline flight. This is because you can't help your child if you can't breathe!

My therapist used a similar analogy. She compared a mother to a pantry that is filled with nutritional food. We are continually giving to our children from our precious pantry of supplies – our time, our energy, our love and our patience. She asked what happens when the pantry is empty, when all of its goodies have been given to our children and there is nothing left. It means that the pantry has nothing left to give. She reminded me that we need to continually restock our pantry in order to give to our children. Replenishing our pantry is all about the importance of self-care. It's about time for ourselves: time to relax, time to be, time to sit in the sunshine with a cup of tea and a good book. It might be time to meditate or be mindful. It might be fun times with our partner, family and friends. It may include special treats – a massage, a manicure or a trip to the beach. Whatever it is that sustains and enriches us.

Having permission to give myself this time was life-changing for me. It went totally against the values that I had been brought up with in my family, which included always putting the other person first. I used to feel guilty if I put myself first. But over the years I have learnt, through hard-won experience, that if I don't make time for myself, I won't have the energy or capacity to give to others. When I feel depleted, whether due to work or home pressures, I need to make time to look after myself. Otherwise, I won't be in the best shape to give to those I care for – my children, my husband, my friends or my clients. And as my wise colleague Gay McKinley reminded me, 'Even Mother Teresa said that she gave from an overflowing bucket, not a rusty, leaky one!'

Talking about how we feel, including the things that we feel anxious about, has an incredible effect on how we think and feel. It helps lighten the burden, so we feel less alone with the problem, and helps to identify and sort things out in your head. Even if you can't resolve the anxiety or the issue in the short term, just talking about how you feel will help. In talking about these things, be discriminating. Choose people who are supportive, understanding, caring and, most importantly, non-judgemental – people who accept you for who you are. Sometimes those people won't be family. Some of us are blessed with family members who are accepting and free of judgement and censure, others are not. You know what kind of family you have and can choose whom you confide in accordingly.

Meditation and mindfulness are two practical strategies that you can turn to every day, to keep yourself emotionally healthy. These are both forms of focused attention. A simple meditation that can be done anytime, anywhere, is to simply focus your attention on your breath, and not engage with any thoughts that come to your mind. And thoughts will come to mind. One thing our mind does constantly is offer up thoughts, thousands of them. The average person has between 12,000 and 60,000 thoughts per day. Unfortunately, eighty per cent of these are negative, and ninety-five per cent are repetitive thoughts.[55] Whatever the exact number, we are constantly thinking, and the majority of our thinking is likely to be unhelpful. I know this by tuning in to my own thoughts and hearing about the thoughts of others. When we are anxious, our thoughts run around in circles repetitively, telling us the same old stories. When this happens, and when we start to notice that we are becoming anxious, or that we are ruminating or worrying, we need to start letting go of our thoughts and focus on the breath (meditation), or on the present moment or our present task (mindfulness).

Mindfulness is about paying attention to the present moment with awareness and without judgement. This means our internal, bodily feelings and any external sensations, such as what we can feel (the warmth of the sun, the coolness of the breeze), hear (birdsong, traffic, aeroplanes, wind) and see (within our visual arena). Mindfulness is also experienced whenever we completely focus on what we are doing. This often occurs naturally when we are doing something we enjoy, such as reading, exercise, art, craft, drawing, colouring in, sewing and other tasks, depending on our personal interests.

Exercise is extremely important and has a direct impact on both anxiety and depression. It fires up the endorphins for a natural feel-good boost. Psychiatrists and psychologists recommend regular exercise as an effective alternative to antidepressants, for less severe forms of anxiety and depression. Always consult with your GP first, for an assessment of your experiences of anxiety and depression, and be guided by your GP on safe and healthy exercise types and levels that are right for you.

CHAPTER 18

DRAWING THE THREADS TOGETHER

Dragonflies symbolise transformation due to the nature of their lifespan – they shed their outer coverings eight to seventeen times during their short lifespan.[56] Having brief lives also makes them symbolic of living in the moment, one way to make the most of our lives. I think, therefore, that the dragonfly is a fitting metaphor for what I have learnt from life, both with and without Simone. Simone was someone who lived her life in the moment. Although at times this frustrated me, I now see it as a better way to live. The dragonfly also symbolises the way my life has been transformed as a result of losing Simone.

There is much that I hoped to convey by telling the story of Simone and me. Yet my overarching purpose was to highlight what I consider to be my most important life lesson: the supreme worth of unconditional love and acceptance, both for our children and for ourselves. If you take away only one message from the book, this is it. Take hold of the concept of unconditional acceptance and love, and allow it to change your life and your relationships, not only with your children, but also with all the important people in your life – your partner, your parents, your siblings, your friends and, most importantly, with yourself. *Love and acceptance are essential* …

Love and accept your child, unconditionally, *no matter what*. Let this be your guiding principle. In every experience, no matter how difficult, express that love, not in mere words alone, but by all your behaviours and attitudes. I have learnt this lesson in the hardest way possible, by losing Simone. If I could relive my relationship with Simone – if I had the proverbial magic wand, or a miracle occurred and I could go back to the time when Simone was born – there are a multitude of things I could and would do differently. The list would probably be endless, but I think you have a fair idea of what it would contain after reading this book.

Most importantly, I would change my attitude towards Simone. I would hold on to the feeling of miraculous wonder that I felt at Simone's birth; I would hold tight to my love for her, borne from that first day, when I held her in my arms. From that day forward, I would love and accept Simone, unconditionally, whatever happened. Instead of focusing on the impact of her behaviour on me, I would take the focus off me and my struggles, and focus on cherishing her, exactly as she was, as she grew and developed, and became the person she was meant to be. I would seek to understand her, rather than criticise, judge or condemn her. I would recognise her as a unique individual, not as some faulty reflection of myself.

I feel as though this was a crucial missing element in my relationship with Simone: I failed to love and accept her for her 'Simoneness'. Rather than seeing her as an individual in her own right, I perceived her to be an extension of me, an extension that contained many parts of myself that I didn't like. I also saw her as a diagnosis – a child with ADHD, as opposed to just unconditionally loving and accepting her. Yet this is the most important birthright for each and every one of us.

Of course, love and acceptance does not diminish or undermine a parent's role in placing limits on our children's behaviour. It is a fundamental part of the parenting role to prioritise our children's wellbeing and safety, to guide and support them to become responsible, law-abiding individuals. There are boundaries and rules that every child needs to learn from their parents as they mature, to enable them to be independent and resilient, to care for themselves and others.

I also know, from life experience, that if Simone had lived there would have continued to be times when her behaviour would have frustrated me. She wasn't an easy person. She was not perfect, and neither am I. There would have been times when I was triggered by my own vulnerabilities, by my own imperfect experiences of being parented. I am not an easy person either, nor am I a perfect parent. What would be different is that I would take the time to acknowledge disagreements between us, reflect upon them, learn from them, apologise to Simone and continue to love and accept her, regardless. I would see our squabbles as Simone being Simone, and me being me. Two different, imperfect people who love each other. I would forgive her and forgive myself.

Sadly, none of us can change the past or the way we may have parented our children. We can, however, change the present (the here-and-now moment), which, ultimately, is all we ever have. If we can provide unconditional love and acceptance to our children, in this moment, we can transform the futures of our children and the relationships that we have with them. I would also argue that this will assist us to transform the relationship that we have with ourselves.

My second most important message is to love and accept yourself unconditionally. This is crucial, and achieving the most important principle (loving your children and others unconditionally) is dependent on it. Without self-love and self-acceptance, you cannot be the clear mirror that reflects your love to your child. It's like Whitney Houston's famous song, 'Greatest Love of All'.[57] If we are unable to love and accept ourselves, unconditionally – just as we are, imperfect though we may be – we cannot fully love and accept our children. The two principles are interdependent.

If I could have given myself unconditional love and acceptance, I am certain that I would have had a much happier and healthier relationship with Simone. Of course, if I had received unconditional love and acceptance myself as a child, it would have been much easier. Yet that wasn't my experience, so I had to learn it the hard way, through the experience of immense regret. At least I have learnt it, even if it has taken a whole lot of living and years of therapy to fully acknowledge and implement it.

The final breakthrough in my personal healing happened in 2019. I finally got it. (About bloody time, I hear you say!) I finally saw what others had been telling me for years; I finally realised that it was my self-flagellation, my constant self-criticism, my harshness towards myself and my lack of self-acceptance that was the cause of all my pain. Instead of helping me, it had made all my problems worse. I realised that it had to stop, that I needed to love and accept myself, just as I was. That I am good enough, simply being me. That I can *just be* Connie.

When I read Gay McKinley's book, *On Becoming Good Enough*,[58] I found the language to express what good enough is really all about. Gay states:

Good Enough is a homecoming. It is a place of rest, a haven; but it is never passive or stagnant. It is vibrant and alive and, at the same time, still and quiet. It is calm, yet excited and proud, but it is never arrogant or superior. It is honest and familiar. It is neither complacent nor substandard, but it is the most generous, loving and demanding sense of true self. There is definitely nothing mediocre about it.

This has certainly been my experience of accepting myself as good enough. While it does feel a peaceful and honest place, it is not the mediocre place I had always feared. I thought that to give up on my sense of not being good enough would mean coming to a grinding halt, accepting defeat, being nothing. Instead, being good enough is a place of continued learning and growth. And in the process of conquering my inner critic, I smashed down the prison walls that had created my experience of depression.

Finally, there was peace, inner peace. I have learnt so much on my journey: understanding, compassion and empathy, and the ability to support and encourage my children's and others' experiences of anxiety, depression, sadness and grief. I have learnt how to look after myself and my black dog.

This monumental change, to self-acceptance, also enabled me to completely change direction in my life. Instead of ruminating on my flaws and berating myself, I was able to make practical, real-life changes. I started to take responsibility for times when I have done wrong, and to right wrongs where I could. I take action every day to make real in my own life what I have learnt from both reading and hard-won personal experience.

Working in the counselling field has also enabled me to deepen my knowledge and self-awareness. Through my work with Relationships Australia, I was ashamed to recognise that I had alternated between passive, passive–aggressive and aggressive communication with my family. I learnt that I needed to be courageous and to speak more assertively, in order to change this pattern of communication. I also discovered, through my supervision process with Catholic Care, that I often operated from either a victim or a rescuer position. I needed to remove myself from both positions, accepting and asserting my vulnerability in some situations and allowing individuals to solve their own problems in others. Making these changes has not been a quick or easy process and has required forgiveness of both myself and others. It has required ongoing practice. It has required having my head, heart and spirit in alignment. And it has required trust – in God, in others and in myself.

Writing this book has been incredibly healing. It has enabled me to set down my thoughts and feelings on paper, and to put much of Simone's life and my own into context. It has helped to heal me, on many different levels. While I will never completely recover from losing Simone, somewhere amid writing this book I realised that I have learnt to accept and live with her loss. It was a quiet and gentle revelation.

I have also learnt that I am strong and resilient. I resonate with the image of a willow tree – while I can bend and sway in the wind and the storms, I will not break. There is a strong core inside me that is stubbornly determined to survive. And I want to give credit where credit is due: thank you, Mum; you gave me that strength. I am a stronger person than I thought I was, I know this now.

I have made peace with Simone and I have made peace with myself, within myself. Through understanding my life with her and without her, I have become a new person; I have been transformed. Simone's life and death were the catalyst for my greatest life lessons: to love and forgive myself; to love and accept others; to navigate the complex, interconnecting landscape of self, parenting and relationships, including grief and loss.

Simone, I have learnt that while I made mistakes in parenting you, you had already forgiven me, long ago. It was me that wasn't able to forgive myself. Now I have. This book is for you, Simone. It is my gift to you, to thank you for all that you have taught me. Farewell, Simone, till we meet once more, at heaven's gate.

APPENDIX A

PRACTICAL SUGGESTIONS

- **Give yourself a break.** Recognise that you, too, are human and therefore fallible. There is no such thing as a perfect mother or a perfect human being. It is part of the human condition to fail and stuff up. *It is normal!*

- **Look after yourself.** For me, it's sitting in the sun and reading a good book, or relaxing with my daughter, or watching a movie, or time with friends – on the phone, at a cafe, at home. For you, it may be picking some flowers from the garden or treating yourself with a nice bunch of flowers. It may be having a massage, a manicure or a pedicure – whatever it is that comforts you. Don't forget that human touch is incredibly healing. Go for a walk, get outside, get physical. Research has proven that a good workout is just as effective as an antidepressant.[*]

---

[*] Seek medical advice from your GP if you are suffering from acute anxiety or depression (if your symptoms are interfering with your daily life).

- **Seek support.** There are various ways you can seek support from a mental health professional.

Life coach

The focus of a life coach will be action-oriented, helping you to work towards your goals or achieve desired behaviours. They are helpful for people who are generally coping well with life, who are simply in need of some support and encouragement to reach their goals. Usually, a life coach will have at least completed some short courses at a coaching college.

Professional counsellor

A professional counsellor has completed university or college qualifications in counselling. They are regulated by accreditation from a counselling organisation, such as the Psychotherapy and Counselling Federation of Australia (PACFA). However, not everyone who calls themselves a counsellor belongs to an association. (It is not a registered name, as the term psychologist is.) So, it is important to confirm that the counsellor *is* a registered member of an accredited organisation.

A good counsellor will create a safe and supportive space for you to explore who you are and what you want in life. They help you to identify and solve your problems. Clients who are struggling with anxiety, depression, grief and loss or relationship issues would benefit from seeing a counsellor. Counselling focuses on matters that are happening in the here-and-now of a person's life. They work to empower clients to make choices that are right for them, through a problem-solving approach.

Psychotherapist

A psychotherapist has training in exploring issues in a client's past, including their childhood and their past adult experiences. Psychotherapy focuses on the conscious, subconscious and unconscious aspects of our inner selves, in particular the relationship we have with our inner self and why.

Psychologist

A psychologist has completed a degree in psychology, combining at least four years of university studies with clinical registration, plus an additional two years of supervised practice, Masters or PhD studies. A clinical psychologist is trained using a scientific, evidence-based approach to solving a client's issues.

Psychiatrist

A psychiatrist is a medical doctor who has specialised in postgraduate psychological training. They are the only professional in the field who can prescribe pharmaceutical medications. They may also provide counselling and/or psychotherapy., They tend to work primarily with patients who have serious mental health conditions, such as severe clinical depression, post-traumatic stress disorder (PTSD), eating disorders, obsessive–compulsive disorder (OCD), schizophrenia, bipolar disorder, borderline personality disorder, narcissistic disorder and antisocial personality disorder.

You don't need a referral from a GP in order to see a psychotherapist, counsellor or life coach. However, to see a psychologist or psychiatrist, you will need a referral and you will be able to claim a Medicare rebate.

I would stress the importance of making sure that there is a good fit between you and your mental health professional. If, after a few sessions, you are not feeling comfortable, or you don't feel a connection or a sense of genuinely being heard and seen, don't hesitate to see another person instead. In the same way that you would change your doctor or hairdresser if you are not satisfied with their level of service, changing your mental health professional is your prerogative.

Talking about how you feel helps you to heal on the inside. When I speak to clients who are suffering greatly, it is often because they feel too guilty and ashamed to talk about how they are feeling, or for some reason the act of expressing their feelings seems unacceptable. Yet the simple act of talking about what you are experiencing can bring enormous relief. Naturally, be selective in who you choose, confiding in safe, non-judgemental, caring people who 'get' you.

- **Write about your feelings.** Journalling is such a healing and helpful practice. I recommend Stephanie Dowrick's excellent book on journal writing.[59] I have recently begun to follow Julia Cameron's advice in her book, *The Artist's Way*,[60] to start each day by writing three morning pages. These are strictly stream-of-consciousness longhand writing, which enables you to clear your mind by putting on the page all your rambling, ruminative thoughts. A lovely resource I found recently is called *Note to Self*,[61] which comprises cards with questions that are designed to develop self-awareness; they help you to clarify goals, make good decisions and live 'an examined life'.

- **Join a support group.** This may be a community group, a book club, a gardening club, a parenting group, a playgroup or a hobby/craft group. Talking to other people will help you to feel less alone.

- **Attend a parenting course (if you are a parent).** There is a wealth of parenting courses available, often run by non-governmental agencies or community groups. There is 1-2-3 Magic for young children, Tuning Into Teens, and Circle of Security is an excellent program that teaches the importance of attachment needs.

- **Extend self-compassion to yourself.** Be kind and generous to yourself, the way you would be to your best friend, husband or child. Kristin Neff has devoted her career in psychology to the art of self-compassion. Self-compassion has distinct differences from self-esteem; it is a judgement-free way of showing understanding and sympathy towards our own failings and imperfections. Brené Brown is another researcher who has written about the importance of accepting our flaws, referring to them as gifts. When accepted and integrated, they lead to wholehearted living and a practice of positive self-worth.

APPENDIX B

MENTAL HEALTH FIRST AID SKILLS AND RESOURCES

- The most important way that you can help someone who is struggling with mental health is through your attitude and presence. Being non-judgemental, authentic and an empathic listener are useful attributes that will help.
- Good listeners provide a space for another person to think through their own ideas and feelings. It's best to offer small, encouraging phrases, such as 'Yes', 'Hmm', 'Okay, I see' and 'Go on, I'm listening', to encourage someone to speak freely. Avoid interrupting by offering your own thoughts or views.
- You can clarify that you have understood what has been spoken by providing a reflection of what you have heard (paraphrasing their words in your own) or a short summary, to ensure that you are correctly understanding what they are aiming to say. Offering this in a tentative way can help someone feel understood.
- Empathic comments such as 'That sounds really tough' or 'I can understand that must be really hard for you', spoken in a genuine, caring manner, can provide comfort.

- You can ask open-ended questions to a gain greater understanding – questions that start with what, how, where or when, as opposed to closed questions that start with do or is. Avoid why questions if you can, because they can easily be perceived as threatening or judgemental, which may increase defensiveness or rationalisations.
- If someone is highly distressed, offer them space to experience their feelings. Sitting alongside someone as they cry, just being present and bearing witness to their pain or sorrow, can be enormously helpful. If appropriate, offer physical comfort – a hand on the arm or leg, an arm around the shoulder, a hug – depending on the nature of the relationship you have with them.
- Avoid giving advice, no matter how well intentioned. Instead, when the person has shared how they are feeling or what the situation is that is troubling, ask them what they need now, or what might help them, or what has helped them in the past. This empowers the individual to come up with their own solutions, which are right for them.
- Sometimes people may ask for your advice or opinion directly. Offer these tentatively, within a framework of: 'This has helped me …' or 'Sometimes doing X has enabled me/provided me with …'
- If a person is highly distressed, they may not be able to think straight. In times of crisis or panic, the cognitive part of our brain goes offline, so they may just need space to breathe and calm down. Going for a walk, sitting together quietly or focusing on the breath may provide sufficient pause to enable them to think more clearly.

If you find yourself in the position of having a suicidal friend or family member, here are some basic skills to guide you:
- Take any threat or discussion of suicide seriously. There is an unfortunate myth circulating that someone who speaks of suicide is only

asking for attention. This is not the case, and has been validated by research.[62]

- Recognise the warning signs of suicidal thinking – talking about wanting to die, expressing feelings of helplessness or depression, saying they are a burden on others. Sudden changes in mood (even happiness after previous sadness), giving away belongings, social withdrawal or reckless behaviour are all indicators of risk.
- Know the danger signs: changes in relationships (separation, divorce, remarriage); loss of partner, family member, friends, home or community; moving to a new school or workplace; changes in financial situation or gambling; excessive use of alcohol and/or drugs; loss of health, either self or family member; unsafe living environment; loss of self-esteem.
- Don't be afraid to ask the question, 'Are you thinking of suicide?' or 'Have you been thinking about taking your own life?' Asking the question will not put the thought in someone's mind. It may already be there; asking may invite the opportunity for discussion.
- Discover if the individual has a plan for how they will take their life. Do they have the means to carry this out? How well prepared is their plan? How long have they been planning the attempt?
- Listen to someone's reason for wanting to die before talking about the reasons they have to live. If you bypass hearing about the pain, you miss a valuable opportunity to understand their experience of suffering. Rushing to provide comfort, solutions or suggestions disempowers the individual and lessens the chance you may have to make a difference.
- Listen carefully for any reasons to live that are already contained within the person's narrative or in their life experience.

- Discover if there have been past suicide attempts. Learn about their mental health history. Do they currently use and/or abuse alcohol or other drugs?
- Does the person have internal resources (personal qualities) or external resources (GP, a mental health practitioner – a psychologist or therapist – friends and/or family members who can support them going forward)?
- Make a safety plan in collaboration with the individual. Disable any current means, such as alcohol, drugs or weapons, by removing them or making them inaccessible.
- As part of the safety plan, carefully list steps to follow if the person either continues to feel suicidal or becomes suicidal again. This should include a list of people, with phone numbers, for the individual to contact if they are feeling unsafe.
- If your friend is in immediate danger, do not leave them alone. Contact the mental health access line of your local hospital or take them to an emergency department.

People to contact. Here is a list of organisations you can call for assistance.[63] All organisations listed are national, unless otherwise stated.

>**1800RESPECT** (1800 737 732) www.1800respect.org.au
>A national sexual assault, family and domestic violence counselling line for anyone who has experienced, or is at risk of, physical or sexual violence.
>
>**Australian Breastfeeding Association** (1800 686 268) www.breastfeeding.asn.au
>Provides breastfeeding information and support to mothers, their support networks and health professionals.

Australian Centre for Grief and Bereavement (1800 642 066) www.grief.org.au
The Australian Centre for Grief and Bereavement is the largest provider of grief and bereavement education in Australia and offers support for Australians who are affected by the difficult emotions associated with loss.

Beyond Blue (1300 224 636) www.beyondblue.org.au
Provides information and support for everyone in Australia, to enable their best possible mental health.

Black Dog Institute (02 9382 4530) www.blackdoginstitute.org.au
The Black Dog Institute and the Australian Institute of Sport (AIS) have partnered to deliver services to build the mental health, wellbeing and resilience of young Australians. They also focus on research, suicide prevention, depression and other mental health conditions. This is not a crisis telephone service, but phone, email and postal inquiries are welcome.

Blue Knot Helpline (1300 657 380) www.blueknot.org.au
Offers free, specialist counselling support and a referral service for people with disability, their families and carers.

Domestic Violence Crisis Service (DVCS) (1800RESPECT) www.dvcs.org.au
For crisis counselling, support and referral to safe accommodation. The crisis line provides crisis intervention, advocacy, referral, information, support and practical assistance for people subjected to, or using, violence and abuse in relationships. The crisis line gives priority to those subjected to violence. (ACT only for some services.)

Family Relationship Advice Line (1800 050 321) www.familyrelationships.gov.au
Provides information on family relationship issues and advice on parenting arrangements after separation.

GriefLine (1300 845 745) www.griefline.org.au

Provides support to people experiencing loss and grief, at any stage in life.

Headspace (1800 650 890) www.headspace.org.au

A free and confidential telephone and online service for young people aged twelve to twenty-five.

Karitane Careline (1300 227 464) www.karitane.com.au

Provides support, advice and encouragement to parents with children up to five years of age. Child and family health nurses are available to discuss feeding problems, immunisation, toilet training, developmental milestones and more. (NSW only.)

Kids Helpline (1800 551 800) www.kidshelpline.com.au

Provides confidential telephone and online counselling services to young people aged five to twenty-five years, for any reason.

Lifeline (13 11 14) www.lifeline.org.au

General and crisis telephone counselling, information and referral services, provided by trained volunteers, supported by professional staff.

MensLine Australia (1300 789 978) www.mensline.org.au

A telephone and online counselling service for men with family and relationship concerns.

Men's Referral Service (1300 766 491) www.ntv.org.au

Offers a confidential telephone service, as well as an online chat service. For men who have been or are behaving in an abusive way, family members who are impacted, and friends, family or colleagues who want to understand how to support abusive men.

Mind Carer Helpline (1300 554 660) www.mindaustralia.org.au

Provides free, confidential information, support and referral for family, carers and friends of people with a mental illness.

PANDA (Perinatal Anxiety and Depression Australia)

(1300 726 306) www.panda.org.au

Provides confidential counselling, support, information and referrals to local services for anyone affected by prenatal, perinatal or postnatal anxiety and depression.

Parent Line (1300 130 052) www.parentline.org.au

Professional counsellors with experience helping families who offer advice and information for parents and carers. Support is available for issues such as behavioural and emotional problems, discipline, adolescent issues, family relationships, single-parent issues, school problems, child care and juvenile justice. (NSW only.)

Pregnancy, Birth & Baby (1800 882 436)

www.pregnancybirthbaby.org.au

Offers free and confidential support and information about pregnancy, infancy and children up to five years of age.

Red Nose Grief and Loss (1300 308 307)

www.rednosegriefandloss.com.au

A free bereavement support line for anyone affected by the unexpected death of a baby or child during birth, pregnancy or infancy, regardless of the cause. A trained volunteer parent is available to chat, advocate and assist with support and services.

Samaritans (135 247) www.thesamaritans.org.au

Provides anonymous crisis support, for issues such as relationship or family problems, loss and bereavement, financial or job-related worries, illness, addiction and suicide. (NSW only.)

SANE (1800 187 263) www.sane.org
Provides information, guidance and referrals to people who are affected by or need support to manage mental health concerns.

Suicide Call Back Service (1300 659 467) www.suicidecallbackservice.org.au
Provides telephone, video and online counselling to people fifteen years and older who are affected by suicide. This can include feeling suicidal, being worried about or caring for someone who is (or may be) suicidal, being bereaved by suicide or supporting people affected by suicide.

Tresillian (1300 272 736) www.tresillian.org.au
Qualified child and family health nurses provide advice on any aspect of parenting for children aged up to five years. (NSW, Victoria and the ACT.)

Wellways (1300 111 400) www.wellways.org
A peer-led, volunteer support and referral service that provides information to people experiencing mental health issues, as well as their families and friends. (Services available in the ACT, NSW, Queensland, Tasmania and Victoria.)

ACKNOWLEDGEMENTS

With heartfelt thanks to my husband Tony for his constant love, care and support. Thank you for giving me the time and freedom over many years to write this book. Thanks for being a listening and encouraging ear, and a calm and gentle presence.

And to our beautiful children, Daniel, Laura and Matthew. And their partners, Bella and Kieran. With all of my love and appreciation for who you are and the joy that you have brought to my life. May you know how much you are unconditionally loved and accepted.

To my family, Dad, John, Shivaun, Peggy, Roy, Jane and John, for your constant love, support and encouragement.

To Gay McKinley, friend, colleague and writing mentor. With heartfelt thanks and gratitude for your encouragement, support and guidance in helping me to shape my story and bring it to life. You have been enormously generous with your time and assistance. Words cannot express how much I am indebted to you. Without you, this book would never have come to fruition.

You believed in me and my story at times when I didn't believe in it myself. For reading, editing and commenting on countless versions, until this final account – thank you!

To Karlie Carroll, my gifted therapist for many years. With heartfelt thanks and gratitude for all you have taught me. Without you, I wouldn't have been able to identify, understand, process and heal all the pieces of my life's journey and, ultimately, write my story.

To Eileen Reeks, my gifted therapist, colleague and spiritual director. With heartfelt thanks and gratitude for all you have taught me in so many different ways. Without you, I would not have been able to sort through the puzzle of my life and, finally, find healing.

To Alison Fraser, with huge thanks and gratitude, who has brought my book to life. Alison, your wisdom, knowledge and experience have been amazing. Thank you for helping me to shape, prune and develop this story into a published book! You have been so kind, gentle, generous and supportive. Your skills, ideas and wonderful way with words have given my story the freshness and directness it needed. You helped me to value my own words above the words of others, whom I had trusted and esteemed more. That is a most invaluable gift that you have imparted to me.

To Kathleen Murphy and Susan Loch, who led me to Alison, who made the dream of my book a reality.

To Cheryl Hingley and Lliane Clarke for your invaluable guidance and editorial assistance. To Joanne Buckley, for your beautiful and artistic cover design.

Acknowledgements

To all my friends and family, who have offered encouragement and interest as I dreamed, talked about and wrote this book, over many years, I am immensely grateful. A special thanks to those who took the time to read it and provide feedback, suggestions and advice – Libby, Karen, Beaté, Sonya, Alexander, Jane, Sue Olds, Sam Forbes and Valerie.

To my past employers and colleagues – Lifeline, Anglicare, Relationships Australia (Illawarra office), Hopefield, Catholic Cemeteries & Crematoria, Catholic Care and Relationships Australia (Sydney office). Thanks to each and every one of you. Your encouragement and belief in me kept me going through the tough times.

To all the wonderful friends, work colleagues (past and present), church family, acquaintances – you know who you are – who supported me and my family as we travelled through our grief journey – thank you. I will be grateful for eternity.

ABOUT THE AUTHOR

Connie Easterbrook is a professional counsellor. She holds a Bachelor of Social Science from Southern Cross University, a Graduate Certificate in Emotionally Focused Therapy and a Certificate IV in Assessment and Workplace Training. Over the past eighteen years, Connie has held positions at Lifeline, Anglicare, Relationships Australia and Catholic Care. She has also provided training to TAFE, St Mark's National Theological Centre, community groups and churches.

About the author

Given Connie's personal experiences, she chose to work in the grief and loss field for many years, assisting individuals and agencies. She provided training, facilitated support groups, and spoke publicly about both suicide postvention, and grief and loss.

My Daughter, Myself is Connie's first book, written in response to her grief following the tragic death of her daughter, Simone, at the age of twenty-one. In 2016, Connie's short story 'Big Grief' was published in the Hunter Writers Centre publication, *Grieve*.

Connie currently runs a small private practice; she also works as a counsellor and relationship educator for Relationships Australia. She lives in the Sutherland Shire with her husband, Tony, her youngest son, Matthew, and their naughty puppy, Bailey.

RECOMMENDED READING LIST

These are books that I have found to be helpful and interesting. I have included the titles of some books that I mention throughout the story, as well as others. Books that have Christian content or are written from a Christian perspective I have marked with a (C).

Books About ADHD

EM Hallowell & JJ Ratey, *Delivered from Distraction,* Ballantine Books, New York, 2006.

EM Hallowell & J J Ratey, *Driven to Distraction,* Random House (Anchor Books), New York, 1994.

S Solden, *Women with Attention Deficit Disorder*, Underwood Books, California, 2005.

Books About Anger

LO Engelhardt & K Katafiasz, *Anger Therapy*, Abbey Press Publications, Indiana, 1985.

H Lerner, *The Dance of Anger*, William Morrow, New York, 1985.

Books About Anxiety

B Aisbett, *The Book of It*, HarperCollins, Sydney, 2008.

B Aisbett, *Fixing It*, HarperCollins, Sydney, 2013.

D Rowe, *Beyond Fear*, Harper Perennial, 2007.

M Wehrenberg, *The 10 Best-Ever Anxiety Management Techniques*, W.W. Norton, New York, 2008.

S Wilson, *First, We Make the Beast Beautiful*, Pan Macmillan, Sydney, 2017.

Books About Christianity

B Bangley, *If I'm Forgiven, Why Do I Still Feel Guilty*, Harold Shaw Publishers, Illinois, 1992. (C)

CS Lewis, *The Problem of Pain*, HarperCollins (William Collins), London, 2012. (C)

B Manning, *The Rabbi's Heartbeat*, NavPress, Colorado, 2003. (C)

TJ Oord, *God Can't*, SacraSage Press, Idaho, 2019. (C)

TJ Oord, *The Uncontrolling Love of God*, InterVarsity Press, Illinois, 2015. (C)

D Tomlinson, *The Bad Christian's Manifesto*, Hodder & Stoughton, London, 2015. (C)

D Tomlinson, *How to be a Bad Christian*, Hodder & Stoughton, London, 2012. (C)

W van der Hart & R Waller, *The Guilt Book*, InterVarsity Press, Illinois, 2014. (C)

D Wilkerson, *Have You Felt Like Giving Up Lately*, Revell, Michigan, 1980. (C)

Books About Counselling/Psychology

S Anderson, *The Journey from Abandonment to Healing*, Penguin (Putnam), New York, 2014.

EN Aron, *The Highly Sensitive Person*, HarperCollins (Element), London, 1999.

E Berne, *Games People Play*, Penguin Books, London, 2010.

J Clear, *Atomic Habits*, Penguin Random House, New York, 2018.

SR Covey, *The 7 Habits of Highly Effective People*, Simon & Schuster, New York, 2004.

D Ford, *Why Good People Do Bad Things*, HarperCollins (Harper One), New York, 2008.

R Harris, *The Happiness Trap*, Exisle Publishing, Wollombi, 2007.

R Harris, *The Reality Slap*, Exisle Publishing, Wollombi, 2011.

TA Harris, *I'm OK – You're OK*, Arrow Books, London, 2012.

J Izzo, *The Five Secrets You Must Discover Before You Die*, Berret Koehler Publishers, San Francisco, 2008.

F Ostaseski, *The Five Invitations*, Flat Iron Books, New York, 2017.

MS Peck, *The Road Less Travelled*, Ebury Publishing, London, 2008.

Books About Depression

B Aisbett, *Taming the Black Dog*, HarperCollins, Sydney, 2000.

H Cloud, *Changes That Heal*, Zondervan, Michigan, 1990. (C)

S Edelman, *Change Your Thinking*, ABC Books, Sydney, 2017.

T Moore, *Dark Nights of the Soul*, Piatkus Books, London, 2004.

D Rowe, *Depression*, Routledge, Oxfordshire, 2003.

Books About Grief

M Devine, *It's OK That You're Not OK*, Sounds True, Colorado, 2017.

L Hone, *Resilient Grieving*, The Experiment, New York, 2017.

HS Kushner, *When Bad Things Happen to Good People*, Pan Books, London, 1981. (C)

JH Lord, *No Time for Goodbyes*, Pathfinder Publishing, California, 2000.

M McKissock & D McKissock, *Coping with Grief*, ABC Books, Sydney, 1995.

B Noel & PD Blair, *I Wasn't Ready to Say Goodbye*, Sourcebooks, Illinois, 2008.

TA Rando, *How To Go On Living When Someone You Love Dies*, Bantam Books, New York, 1988.

J Samuel, *Grief Works*, Penguin Life, UK, 2017.

J Samuel, *This Too Shall Pass*, Penguin Life, UK, 2020.

HN Wright, *Recovering from Losses in Life*, Revell, Michigan, 2006. (C)

Personal Stories of Grief and Loss

M Beattie, *The Grief Club*, Hazelden, Minnesota, 2006.

U Glennon, *Ciara's Gift*, UWA Publishing, Crawley, 2010.

K Lang, *Courage*, InHouse Publishing, Queensland, 2016.

S Loch, *Jessica's Gift*, Book Therapy, Sydney, 2020.

J Newling, *Missing Christopher*, Allen & Unwin, Sydney, 2014.

L Van Der Horst, *Without My Mum*, Schwartz Publishing (Nero), Victoria, 2016.

Grief after Suicide Bereavement

S Clark, *After Suicide*, Hill of Content, Melbourne, 1995.

M Linn-Gust, *Do They Have Bad Days in Heaven?*, Chellehead Works, Albuquerque, 2001.

AD Wolfelt, *Understanding Your Suicide Grief*, Companion Press, Colorado, 2009.

Books About Journal Writing

J Cameron, *The Artist's Way*, Macmillan, London, 2016.

S Dowrick, *Creative Journal Writing*, Allen & Unwin, Crows Nest, 2007.

Books About Near Death and/or Heavenly Experiences

T Burpo, *Heaven Is For Real*, Thomas Nelson, Tennessee, 2010. (C)

BJ Eadie, *Embraced by the Light*, HarperCollins (Element), London, 2003. (C)

A & F Kramarik, *Akiane*, Thomas Nelson, Tennessee, 2006. (C)

D Piper, *90 Minutes in Heaven*, Revell, Michigan, 2004. (C)

Books About Parenting

S Biddulph, *Raising Boys*, Finch Publishing, Sydney, 1997.

S Biddulph, *Raising Girls*, Finch Publishing, Sydney, 2013.

DR Campbell, *How to Really Love Your Child*, Victor Books, London, 1977. (C)

DR Campbell, *How to Really Love Your Teen*, Victor Books London, 1981. (C)

G Chapman, *The 5 Love Languages of Teenagers*, Moody Press, Chicago, 2017.

G Chapman & R Campbell, *The 5 Love Languages of Children*, Moody Press, Chicago, 2016.

D Corkville Briggs, *Your Child's Self-Esteem*, Broadway Books, New York, 1970.

A Faber & E Mazlish, *How to Talk So Kids Will Listen & Listen So Kids Will Talk*, Templar Publishing, London, 2012.

A Faber & E Mazlish, *How to Talk So Teens Will Listen & Listen So Teens Will Talk*, Templar Publishing, London, 2006.

J Gottman, *Raising an Emotionally Intelligent Child*, Simon & Schuster, New York, 1997.

B Harris, *When Your Kids Push Your Buttons*, Little Brown (Piatkus), London, 2003.

DJ Siegel & M Hartzell, *Parenting from the Inside Out*, Penguin, New York, 2013.

Books About Self-Acceptance

G McKinley, *On Becoming Good Enough*, Ligare Book Printers, Sydney, 2016.

K Neff, *Self-Compassion*, William Morrow, New York, 2011.

T Simon (editor), *The Self-Acceptance Project*, Sounds True, California, 2016.

H Stone & S Stone, *Embracing Your Inner Critic*, HarperCollins, New York, 1993.

Books About Self-Esteem

N Branden, *The Six Pillars of Self-Esteem*, Bantam Books, New York, 1994.

J Burgo, *Shame*, Skill Path Publications, London, 2018.

D Corkville Briggs, *Your Child's Self-Esteem*, Broadway Books, New York, 1970.

K Katafiasz, *Self-Esteem Therapy*, Abbey Press, Indiana, 1995.

R Ray, *The Art of Self-Kindness*, Pan Macmillan, Sydney, 2019.

Books About Trauma

B Rothschild, *8 Keys to Safe Trauma Recovery*, WW Norton, New York, 2010.

B Van Der Kolk, *The Body Keeps the Score*, Penguin Random House, New York, 2014.

Books by Brené Brown

B Brown, *Daring Greatly*, Penguin, London, 2012.

B Brown, *The Gifts of Imperfection*, Hazelden, Minnesota, 2010.

B Brown, *I Thought It Was Just Me (But It Isn't)*, Penguin, London, 2008.

Books by Glennon Doyle

G Doyle, *Carry On, Warrior*, Simon & Schuster, New York, 2013.

G Doyle, *Love Warrior*, Flat Iron Books, New York, 2016.

G Doyle, *Untamed*, Penguin Random House (Vermillon), London, 2020.

Books by Harriet Lerner

H Lerner, *The Dance of Anger*, William Morrow, New York, 1985.

H Lerner, *The Dance of Connection*, HarperCollins, New York, 2001.

H Lerner, *The Dance of Intimacy*, HarperCollins, New York, 1989.

H Lerner, *The Mother Dance*, HarperCollins, New York, 1998.

Books by Matthew Johnstone

M Johnstone, *I Had a Black Dog*, Pan Macmillan, Sydney, 2005.

A Johnstone & M Johnstone, *Living with a Black Dog*, Pan Macmillan, Sydney, 2008.

Books by Stephanie Dowrick

S Dowrick, *Choosing Happiness*, Allen & Unwin, Crows Nest, 2003.

S Dowrick, *Creative Journal Writing*, Allen & Unwin, Crows Nest, 2007.

S Dowrick, *Intimacy & Solitude*, Random House Australia, Milsons Point, 1991.

S Dowrick, *The Intimacy & Solitude Self-Therapy Book*, WW Norton, New York, 1993.

S Dowrick, *The Universal Heart*, Penguin, Victoria, 2000.

REFERENCES

1. K Gibran, *The Prophet*, Knopf, New York, 1923.
2. R Atkinson, *The Gift of Stories*, Praeger, Westport, 2000.
3. B Brown, *The Gifts of Imperfection*, Hazelden, Minnesota, 2010.
4. G Doyle, *Untamed*, Penguin Random House (Vermillon), London, 2020.
5. R Karen, *Becoming Attached*, Oxford University Press, New York, 1998.
6. L Van Der Horst, *Without My Mum*, Schwartz Publishing (Nero), Victoria, 2016.
7. EN Aron, *The Highly Sensitive Person*, HarperCollins (Element), London, 1999.
8. D Corkville Briggs, *Your Child's Self-Esteem*, Broadway Books, New York, 1970.
9. K Leman, *The Birth Order Book*, Revell, Michigan, 2004.
10. HN Wright, *The Power of a Parent's Words*, Regal Books, California, 1991.
11. D Olsen, 'Circumflex Model of Marital and Family Systems', *Journal of Family Therapy*, vol. 22/2, 2000, pp. 144–167.
12. DJ Siegel & M Hartzell, *Parenting from the Inside Out*, Penguin, New York, 2013.
13. S Anderson, *The Journey from Abandonment to Healing*, Penguin (Putnam), New York, 2014.
14. G Chapman, *The 5 Love Languages*, Northfield Publishing, Chicago, 2010.
15. P Leach, *Baby and Child*, Penguin, Middlesex, 1977.
16. I Buttrose & P Adams, *Motherguilt*, Penguin (Viking), Victoria, 2005.
17. C Jung, *Memories, Dreams, Reflections: An Autobiography*, HarperCollins, New York, 2019.

18 HJM Nouwen, *The Inner Voice of Love*, Darton, Longman & Todd, London, 1997.
19 Third Day, *Wherever You Are*, Provident Music Group, 2005.
20 Casting Crowns, *The Altar and the Door*, Beachstreet Records, 2007.
21 CL Goforth, 'Dragonflies and the Afterlife', *The Dragonfly Woman*, 2013, viewed 18 March 2019, <https://thedragonflywoman.com/?s=the+afterlife>.
22 W Matthews, 'The Day You Went Away', *Lily*, Rhinoceros Records, 1992.
23 J Jordan & B Baugher, *After Suicide Loss*, Caring People Press, US, 2016.
24 JH Hewett, *After Suicide*, Westminster John Knox Press, Louisville, 1996.
25 'Trichotillomania (hair-pulling disorder)', *Mayo Clinic*, viewed 18 March 2019, <https://www.mayoclinic.org/diseases-conditions/trichotillomania/symptoms-causes/syc-20355188>.
26 K Katafiasz, *Grief Therapy*, Abbey Press, Indiana, 2004.
27 K Katafiasz, *Grief Therapy*, Abbey Press, Indiana, 2004.
28 P Karst, *The Invisible String*, DeVorss & Company, Canada, 2000.
29 KG Nadeau, EB Littman & PO Quinn, *Understanding Girls with ADHD*, Advantage Books, Washington, DC, 2016. S Solden, *Women with Attention Deficit Disorder*, Underwood Books, California, 2005.
30 S Solden, *Women with Attention Deficit Disorder*, Underwood Books, California, 2005.
31 S Solden, *Women with Attention Deficit Disorder*, Underwood Books, California, 2005.
32 KG Nadeau, EB Littman & PO Quinn, *Understanding Girls with ADHD*, Advantage Books, Washington, DC, 2016.
33 Aristotle, *The Art of Rhetoric*, Oxford University Press, UK, 2018.
34 S Dowrick, *The Universal Heart*, Penguin, Victoria, 2000.
35 H Lerner, *The Dance of Anger*, William Morrow, New York, 1985.
36 MA Webster, *Emotion-Focused Counselling*, Annandale Institute, Annandale, 2017.
37 A Miller, 'The Essential Role of an Enlightened Witness in Society', *Alice Miller Child Abuse and Mistreatment*, 1997, viewed 23 March 2019, <https://www.alice-miller.com/en/the-essential-role-of-an-enlightened-witness-in-society/>.
38 S Dowrick, *Intimacy & Solitude*, Random House Australia, Milsons Point, 1991.
39 B Aisbett, *The Book of It*, HarperCollins, Sydney, 2008.
40 S Wilson, *First, We Make the Beast Beautiful*, Pan Macmillan, Sydney, 2017.

41 M Wehrenberg, *The 10 Best-Ever Anxiety Management Techniques*, W.W. Norton, New York, 2008.
42 M Johnstone, *I Had a Black Dog*, Pan Macmillan, Sydney, 2005.
43 A Mierop, *Goodreads Quotes*, viewed 15 March 2019, <https://www.goodreads.com/author/quotes/18758658.Allison_Mierop>.
44 D Rowe, *Beyond Fear*, Harper Perennial, 2007.
45 D Rowe, *Beyond Fear*, Harper Perennial, 2007.
46 MA Webster, *Emotion-Focused Counselling*, Annandale Institute, Annandale, 2017.
47 H Stone & S Stone, *Embracing Your Inner Critic*, HarperCollins, New York, 1993.
48 K Cherry, 'What is Cognitive Dissonance' *Very Well Mind*, 2022, viewed 3 March 2022, <https://www.verywellmind.com/what-is-cognitive-dissonance-2795012>.
49 H Stone & S Stone, *Embracing Your Inner Critic*, HarperCollins, New York, 1993.
50 K Neff, *Self-Compassion*, William Morrow, New York, 2011.
51 T Simon (editor), *The Self-Acceptance Project*, Sounds True, California, 2016.
52 B Harris, *When Your Kids Push Your Buttons*, Little Brown (Piatkus), London, 2003.
53 B Harris, *When Your Kids Push Your Buttons*, Little Brown (Piatkus), London, 2003.
54 A Faber & E Mazlish, *How to Talk So Kids Will Listen & Listen So Kids Will Talk*, Templar Publishing, London, 2012.
55 P Verma, 'Destroy Negativity From Your Mind With This Simple Exercise', *Mission*, 2017, viewed 20 July 2022, <https://medium.com/the-mission/a-practical-hack-to-combat-negative-thoughts-in-2-minutes-or-less-cc3d1bddb3af>.
56 Carlos, 'How Long do Dragonflies Live?', *Learn About Nature*, 2022, viewed 19 July 2022, <https://www.learnaboutnature.com/insects/dragonfly/how-long-do-dragonflies-live/>.
57 W Houston, 'Greatest Love of All', *Whitney Houston*, Sony Music, 1985.
58 G McKinley, *On Becoming Good Enough*, Ligare Book Printers, Sydney, 2016.
59 S Dowrick, *Creative Journal Writing*, Allen & Unwin, Crows Nest, 2007.
60 J Cameron, *The Artist's Way*, Macmillan, London, 2016.
61 G McLean, *Note to Self*, Innovative Resources, Victoria, 2009.
62 'Suicide myths and facts', *Beyond Blue*, viewed 20 July 2022, <https://www.beyondblue.org.au/the-facts/suicide-prevention/myths-and-facts>.

63 Australian Institute of Family Studies, *Helplines, telephone and online counselling services for children, young people and adults: Australia-wide*, CFCA Resource sheet – April 2021, viewed 25 July 2022, < https://aifs.gov.au/sites/default/files/publication-documents/2104_helplines_australia-wide_resource_sheet_0.pdf>.

www.ingramcontent.com/pod-product-compliance
Lightning Source LLC
Chambersburg PA
CBHW040240010526
44107CB00065B/2814